PRAISE FOR

ANCESTRAL GRIMOIRE

"*Ancestral Grimoire* is a phenomenal follow-up to Nancy Hendrickson's previous book, *Ancestral Tarot*. In this new workbook, Hendrickson takes readers on a magical journey where they learn how to construct a personal Book of Shadows filled with ancestral wisdom. Monthly exercises, divination techniques, and rituals will help readers connect with their ancestral roots to manifest the life they want today. I've got a family tree full of scoundrels and ne'er do wells, but Hendrickson shows that even those relatives have wisdom to offer. This is a necessary book for tarot readers, magical folks, and anyone who wants to see how the past can create a new, better future."

—THERESA REED, author of *Twist Your Fate*

"*Ancestral Grimoire* is a hand to hold while exploring your roots. Nancy guides seekers through the magic of divination and personal symbolism to find the basis for our families and our magic. This book is a lighthouse in the dark, bringing safety and comfort to those lost in the sea of ancestor veneration."

—AMY BLACKTHORN, author of *Blackthorn's Protection Magic, Blackthorn's Botanical Magic,* and other books of magic

"Nancy Hendrickson's *Ancestral Grimoire* is a genealogical adventure that will take you on a deep-dive exploration of your innate magic as seen through the scope of ancestral inheritance. If you're looking to deepen your knowledge of self and connect with your ancestors in a brand-new way, this is a must-have for your bookshelf. As a genealogist and magical woman, my foray into the Land of Tarot has been eye-opening and fulfilling, and I can't wait to go back!"

—CAIRELLE CROW, genealogist, owner of *Sacred Roots*, and editor of *Brigid's Light*

"Many witches struggle to identify the magic that lies within their ancestry and to untether themselves from the limitations of genealogical evidence. Nancy Hendrickson's highly personal and detailed system of working with tarot alongside other clarifying techniques can help the uncertain practitioner make a clear start on going deeper with ancestor work. By following her annual cycle of divination and other suggested practices, the reader can work intuitively to create a scrapbook grimoire of their own magical ancestors. Working with ancestors is essential for so many witches, and this book offers a unique way to do just that."

—CHRISTINE GRACE, author of *The Witch at The Forest's Edge* and cohost of the *Betwixt & Between Podcast*

"At last, a contemporary solution for setting up an age-old Book of Shadows. With the option of designing your pages seasonally, monthly, or whenever Spirit moves you, Nancy Hendrickson's *Ancestral Grimoire* takes us through a number of engaging and easy-to-follow techniques to understand and connect with our ancestry while growing our own magick. From tarot to casting and many ancient exercises in between (I'm looking at you, Weather Magic!), *Ancestral Grimoire* is a must for those looking for clear instruction in creating a personal grimoire that deepens with time."

—CARRIE PARIS, creator of *The Relative Tarot*

"Ancestor veneration and the work that goes with it have long been a shadowed practice in much of the West, finding its deepest expression in genealogy and family stories. As we reclaim these powerful, helpful connections, it is so important to have information presented in a way that invites us into these beautiful practices. That's why I am grateful for Nancy Hendrickson's fascinating book, which is well-written and chock-full of practical information. This belongs on your shelf!"

—H. BYRON BALLARD, author of *Seasons of a Magical Life*

"Many of us feel the call of our ancestors but—if we come from a cultural tradition that does not include ancestor work—simply do not know how to begin. This is where Nancy Hendrickson's *Ancestral Grimoire* fills a very large gap. Using a variety of tools, from tarot to runes to charm casting, Hendrickson takes us on a valuable journey where we are part of a long line of those who are clamoring to work with us, if we will only let them. I particularly love the monthly built-in program that considers working with ancestors from every possible angle throughout the year. *Ancestral Grimoire* is written in a way that deepens the practice of someone familiar with ancestor work while also giving brand-new practitioners a beautiful start. Well thought-out and absolutely a delight to use—I could not recommend *Ancestral Grimoire* more."

—JENNA MATLIN, author of *Will You Give Me a Reading?*

"*Ancestral Grimoire* is creative, brilliant, and inspiring! Nancy Hendrickson thoughtfully leads us through the tarot and oracles to meet our ancestors and dive into our magical lineage. Seeing ourselves through the eyes of our ancestors illuminates a deeper sense of inner wisdom. Each month is packed with meaningful journal prompts and spreads to help us discover parts of ourselves that lie deep within. With each step on this path, we peer into these dormant parts of ourselves, seeing our magnificent and potent magic."

—LAURA LOUELLA, author and editor of *Brigid's Light*

"*Ancestral Grimoire* enabled me to develop a personal and healthy ancestral practice—a step far beyond simple DNA research and family tree-building. As a lifelong keeper of journals, sketchbooks, and such, I was surprised by the new depths of insight I was able to achieve using the methods in this book. Your own grimoire will be the bridge that you build toward your ancestors, but this book will provide the sturdy legs for that bridge."

—STACEY WILLIAMS-NG, tarot artist and creator of *The Southern Gothic Oracle*

"The ancestors are a much-misunderstood category of spirits in the modern revival of witchcraft and polytheistic Paganism. Nancy Hendrickson's *Ancestral Grimoire* offers a twelve-month curriculum of divination exercises, illuminating personal ancestral and past-life spirit allies. At the end of a year's practice, diligent witches will have a personalized Book of Shadows that will provide insight for the rest of their magical lives. Highly recommended!"

—CAROLINE KENNER, founder of *The Fool's Dog* tarot and oracular apps company

"Your ancestors love you and want to meet you, but where do you begin a relationship with spirits? Nancy Hendrickson has got you covered. In her brilliant book, *Ancestral Grimoire*, she gives you dozens of hands-on exercises with tarot, pendulums, and omens, as well as an entire year of activities to discover who your ancestors are and what loving messages they have for you. Her tools to connect you to your loved ones who have passed on are simple and easy-to-use, and Nancy's approachable style makes diving into your spiritual lineage a joy. If you've ever wanted to deepen your relationship with those who have gone before you, you will feel their loving closeness through this amazing book. I can't recommend it enough."

—MADAME PAMITA, author of *Madame Pamita's Magical Tarot*, *Baba Yaga's Book of Witchcraft* and *The Book of Candle Magic*

"In *Ancestral Grimoire*, Nancy Hendrickson makes the heady concept of ancestral magic approachable. Her warm, lyrical voice expands the ways we can use tarot to work with our ancestors and find our magic. *Ancestral Grimoire* is a delightful and empowering read that easily teaches profound transformative practices for every season and every seeker. The deeply personal forward by Benebell Wen beautifully prepares us for this magical journey."

—CHRISTIANA GAUDET, author of *Tarot Tour Guide*

"In *Ancestral Grimoire*, Nancy Hendrickson has created yet another roadway of discovery for the magical practitioner. For those committed to doing the work, the rewards include the creation of their own ancestral grimoire—a record of their ancestors, their magic, and the world of divination. Hendrickson has given us the book to take our work with the ancestors to the next level."

—RHONDA ALIN, founder of Northern New Jersey Tarot Meetup

ANCESTRAL GRIMOIRE

Connect with the Wisdom of the Ancestors through Tarot, Oracles, and Magic

NANCY HENDRICKSON

FOREWORD BY
BENEBELL WEN

WEISER BOOKS

This edition first published in 2022 by Weiser Books, an imprint of
Red Wheel/Weiser, LLC
With offices at:
65 Parker Street, Suite 7
Newburyport, MA 01950
www.redwheelweiser.com

ISBN: 978-1-57863-777-5
Library of Congress Cataloging-in-Publication Data available upon request.

The Queens images from *Modern Witch Tarot*, text and illustration © Lisa Sterle, 2019.
First published by (and reproduced with the permission of) Liminal 11 Ltd. All rights
reserved. The Knights from *Bonestone & Earthflesh Tarot* used with permission of Avalon
Cameron (artwork by Ana Tourian) and from *The Relative Tarot* by Carrie Paris, used
with permission. The Pages from *The Robin Wood Tarot*, used with the permission of
Llewellyn Worldwide Ltd. *The Hoodoo Tarot* by Tayannah Lee McQuillar, artwork by
Katelan V. Foisy, published by Inner Traditions International and Bear & Company,
© 2020. All rights reserved. *www.Innertraditions.com*. Reprinted with permission of the
publisher. *Spirit Oracle* by Carrie Paris, used with permission. *Blooming Cat Tarot*, used
with permission of Jen Brown/Cosmic Eye Tarot. Tarot card images of the Waite Deck
reproduced in the text created by Red Wheel/Weiser, LLC.

Cover design by Kathryn Sky-Peck
Interior by Maureen Forys, Happenstance Type-O-Rama
Typeset in Adobe Jenson, ITC Benguiat, and Incognito Pro

Printed in the United States of America
IBI

10 9 8 7 6 5 4 3 2 1

In gratitude to Jessica Macbeth, whose magical
fingerprints are scattered throughout this book.

CONTENTS

FOREWORD

At an hour after sundown, a candle lit, and a choice piece of petrified wood nearby, I shuffle my cards and follow the opening prompt in this book, repeating, "I believe my most potent form of magic is . . ." I then draw a single card.

The Knight of Pentacles. I see my methodical tenacity, a dedication to knowledge—perhaps a trait I inherited from an ancestor. In these pages, you'll learn that a Knight card in a reading doesn't necessarily point to a man; Nancy Hendrickson will share with you her own revelatory experiences where a 16th-century French woman who endured the Inquisition shows up in a reading through the Knight of Pentacles.

From that prelude of a single card preliminary draw, *Ancestral Grimoire* walks the reader through how to commune with ancestors and fleshes out the answer to that initial prompt. Hendrickson is a tarot master and genealogist who has had a keen connection to ancestral work since her girlhood. Preceding *Ancestral Grimoire* was *Ancestral Tarot* published in 2021, which introduced me to dedicated work with different types of ancestors—ancestors of blood, ancestors of place, and ancestors of time. *Ancestral Grimoire* will help to formulate a comprehensive yearlong practicum for deepening a personal ancestral practice.

My father grew up living in a large traditional Chinese-style manor for extended families, where a central hall housed the ancestral altar. Every morning, incense would be lit at the altar, and every evening, the red lacquered plaques of family names were illuminated by consecrated candlelight. If you needed to pray for better fortunes or give a confession and pray for forgiveness, you knelt before your ancestors.

In modern times, having an entire family hall dedicated for honoring ancestors doesn't seem quite as practical. And so a book like *Ancestral Grimoire* becomes the modern-day solution. These pages provide inspiration for how to remember where we come from, for honoring family bonds that transcend space-time, and for integrating our family tree into our spiritual practice.

Following the guidance in this book, I sourced a beautiful blank journal that I dedicated to my ancestral journaling work, acquired a set of pens and colored pencils, and thoughtfully selected a tarot deck and an oracle deck to work with. Throughout these pages, Hendrickson will walk you through twelve months of magic. Not only is this a grimoire for working with ancestors, but you will also be introduced to land spirits, exploring facets of weather magic like rainmaking and wind whistling, learn to read the weather as omens, and work with rattles in past life soul journeys. Day by day, I worked through the card spreads in this book, wrote reflections in my ancestral journal, and deepened my sense of connection to the spirit realm.

In the first month, I commenced my exploration with inherited magic—working with an ancestor who shares my bloodline. Inspired by the text, I shuffled the sixteen Court cards, fanned them out, and drew one card. The Knight of Pentacles again. What were the odds. Synchronicities in tarot readings never cease to fascinate me. You'll learn in this text that the suit of Pentacles and the element Earth correspond with land and prosperity magic. I descend from farmers on my father's side, and I've always had an internal body clock attuned to an agricultural calendar, so my card draw makes perfect sense. Learning that I've inherited a bond with land and prosperity magic through the Knight of Pentacles ancestor resonates deeply. From there, daily draws throughout that first month imparted profound lessons from my blood ancestor, this Knight of Pentacles, developing and honing that inherited magic tied to the land and to prosperity.

If the card you draw from the sixteen Courts is from the suit of Wands, then your inherited power by blood is fire magic. If from the suit of Cups, it's healing magic, and a Court card from the suit of Swords imparts upon you an inherited gift in communication magic—among your blood ancestors are writers, scholars, perhaps even politicians, judges, or diplomats.

The second month of working with *Ancestral Grimoire* will guide you through exploration of personal magic. You'll work with an ancestor who can help you find your own independent calling. Exercises prompt communication and conversation with another ancestor to help you sharpen your visions, so that those visions can become your reality. Rituals and folk magic bring these teachings to life. Hendrickson will teach you how to craft your own manifesting jar to bring to fruition that which you most seek to attain.

At the start of the second month, I shuffled my tarot deck, set an intention to meet an ancestor who could help me optimize my abilities as a manifestor, and drew from the top of the deck, as Hendrickson instructs, until I arrived at a Court card. The very first card I drew was the Knight of Wands. In Chapter 2, Hendrickson tells us that the Knight of Wands is a restless spirit with a magpie attention span, seeking all that glitters. He is also an adventuresome spirit, an explorer. Here, I believe I see my uncle— my mother's brother who passed on when she was in high school. I've never met him, but I see him in this Knight of Wands archetype.

I dedicated the rest of the month connecting to the spirit of this uncle. The Major Arcanum key signifying my uncle's manifestation ability—Key 0: The Fool. I chuckle, because this resonates with what my mother has said about her late brother's personality. MacGregor Mathers describes the Fool card as indicative of atonement and redemption. In Appendix B of this text, the keywords assigned to the Fool are *innocence* and *trust*. Here is a harbinger of a new odyssey to come. The spirit of my uncle will be helping me manifest a new path.

In the third month, you'll explore healing magic, tapping into an Ancient One from millennia ago, in your family line. You'll do daily readings to work with your Ancient One, getting insights and also getting healed. Healing-magic exercises in this book begin with inner-child healing, then work through feelings of loss, grief, trauma, anxiety, and regret. Working with your ancestors will help you to clear blocked energy within your system.

These beautiful exercises connected me both to memories of my grandparents and also to visions of the ancestors I never met. At the close of this twelve-month practicum, you will have a scrapbook or commonplace book of family and even mystical reflections. *Ancestral Grimoire* is a book that will inspire you to inquire about your genealogy, your family history, culture, and heritage, and enrich your sense of personal identity.

After an intensive practicum working through these exercises, you'll be concluding with the same inquiry you started with, now rephrased as an affirmative. "Today, I know my most potent form of magic is . . ." I pull the Three of Cups. This is the joy of community bonds. Today, I know my most potent form of magic is my empathic connection with others. Through the inner journey I endeavored upon while working through *Ancestral Grimoire*, I emerged out the other side having transmuted the Knight of Pentacles into the Three of Cups—my dedication to the work has achieved fruitful ingenuity, and what gifts I have inherited from my lineage I now make my own by sharing with the community this bounty I've created.

Now go find a unique personal journal to dedicate as your Ancestral Grimoire and start selecting the tarot or oracle decks you'll want to work with throughout the coming months. You, dear reader, are about to embark on a rarefied spiritual and even mystical journey.

BENEBELL WEN, AUTHOR OF *HOLISTIC TAROT*

ACKNOWLEDGMENTS

I'm fortunate to be surrounded by so many magical people. Without them, I'm not sure I could have juggled quite so many ancestors in a single book. Thanks especially to Fred, John, and Patti for keeping me on as even a keel as possible. Sorry about those days I fell out of the boat.

Also, boundless gratitude to my friends who tested spreads and theories. They told me what they liked, what worked, and when I needed to be much clearer. Thank you, Cheri Fritzley, Dee Di Benedictis, Holly Fowler, Jennie Reece, Jessica de Vreeze, Kyle Miller, and TeriAnne Huffman. Thanks also to Amber Highland and the gang at *The Cartomancer Magazine* for their unwavering support of my ancestral work. And eternal gratitude to the many readers of *Ancestral Tarot*—your kind emails and comments gave me the heart to do a deep dive into ancestral magic. I also want to give a shout-out to all you indie deck creators, especially Carrie Paris, Jen Brown, and Avalon Cameron. Tarot, through your eyes, is an evolving art form for which I'm most grateful.

And of course, a special thanks to Judika Illes, a superb editor and an unwavering advocate. May your days be blessed.

Lastly, thanks to my family, both past and present. They may not know tarot or believe in magic, but they do believe in me.

INTRODUCTION

*H*ave you ever started a project without knowing how it ends? That was me on February 1, when I wrote the first words of this book. Although I didn't know how it would unfold, I knew it needed to be written.

What I remember most about that morning was opening the door and hearing two crows chattering off in the west, while in the east a flock of sparrows chirped a greeting. As mythology tells us, the crow can simultaneously see past, present, and future—and the sparrow is the guardian of ancestral knowledge. So it was no coincidence that both flew in that morning. For all the things I didn't know, there was one I did: Magic was afoot.

Crow and sparrow appeared time and again during the months I was writing. Their cackle and chirp nudged me further and further into a world where the extraordinary was as natural as the turning of the seasons—a world where magical ancestors were waiting to remind me of this most powerful truth:

We are born magicians, who have forgotten our magic.

At some point, as children, we learned that an unseen playmate was imaginary, that unicorns never trod the Earth, and giants were only a thing of legend and lore. Our magical ancestors say otherwise. Your childhood friend may have been invisible but not imaginary, and yes, unicorns did frolic in the forest, while giants roamed the planet.

Even more, we all have ancestors who knew how to work with weather, dream the future, and prepare herbs that healed and food that lasted far beyond our paltry "sell by" dates. They could communicate with the little people, the nature spirits, their own ancestors, the trees, the animals, and the sea. Being magical was simply working within the framework of their natural abilities.

About now you might be thinking, "Well, yeah, that may be *your* ancestors but not mine." Not so. If you're drawn to this work, if you're holding this book, your ancestors were as magical as mine. What I'm asking is that you suspend your adult logic for a couple hundred pages and give me a chance to prove it.

I'm inviting you to venture with me into a land your magical ancestors knew well. There, the supernatural was natural. It was a time when we looked to the stars to interpret our dreams and to the birds to fly out during the day and return at night with news of other lands. It was a time when smoke carried prayers, and running brooks their wishes. If you stick with me, as you read the last word on the last page, you will know your own magic.

If you know me in real life or on Instagram, you might wonder how this Virgo could be walking a path so lacking in logic or practicality. The truth is, my Aquarius rising has always known that cultural influences have convinced us to only see the world through the eyes of hard evidence. If we can't see it or touch it, it doesn't exist, right? So much for those unicorns.

But what if—once upon a time—we knew how to see across dimensions? Or we could pick up vibrations as easily as we could pick up a stone? And we knew how to hear that stone's message? I believe our magical ancestors could do all this because no one told them they couldn't.

Magic—in its many forms—is real, and this book is going to show you how to find and work with your ancestors who had those magical skills and now share them with you.

You will learn how to use tarot, runes, pendulums, and other forms of divination to connect across the centuries. You will follow the path of the unknown, as you chart your own magical future.

Above all, you will learn how to live life with your energy receivers turned on.

If you're wondering how to work with ancestors you never knew, I get it. How can you gain insight or trust solutions from people without names or faces? The truth is, of the millions of your direct ancestors, you only knew a handful. In this, we're all in the same boat.

In our time together, you're going to meet at least twelve of your magical ancestors. Along the way, you'll save their knowledge, as well as your own, in an Ancestral Grimoire. There, you'll chronicle the ancestral communications, divination experiences, magical traditions, and wisdom of each. They will guide you through the cycles of time in a way that's personal to you and no one else.

Not all will have the same magic as yours. But one or two may hold the key to that magical portal you've been seeking.

At the close of each month, you will have accumulated valuable knowledge about the magical paths walked by your family. At the end of a year—or less, if you choose—you will know without a doubt that their power is your power, and their magic is yours.

This is not a book of magical spells or casting circles. My experience in working with the ancestors is via the magic of energy and—most often—the use of tarot to interpret that energy. If you use crystals, spells, candles, herbs, or other magical tools, please know that they overlay beautifully with the energy magic you'll be using throughout this book. If you feel called to add one of your own tools, please do; the magic you work will be all the more powerful. Combined, you'll make an energetic connection to the past that will shape your future.

The cliff is ahead, the Divine Fool is prepared, and I'm with you all the way. If you're ready to jump, there's just one more thing to do.

BEFORE YOU BEGIN

You will need a deck of cards.

Ancestral Grimoire is built around the practices that will help you find your personal magic, so it's most important to understand two things before even beginning.

I'm going to talk about your grimoire in Chapter 1, but until you start one, just note the answers to the following.

First, answer the prompt below. If you don't have a clue about your magic, that's okay.

On this very first day of working with *Ancestral Grimoire*, I believe my most potent form of magic is _____
_____.

Second, why are you here?

It's a simple question, but a multilayered one. Draw a single tarot or oracle card to answer. This will go in your grimoire as well.

HOW TO USE THIS BOOK

Part I: Tools for Divination

Part I contains information on all of the tools you'll be using in your grimoire. These include the Court cards, pendulums, runes, oracles, charms, sigils, and Lenormand. You'll also learn the importance of setting up your grimoire and whether you want to work with the months, seasons, or sabbats. If you're already a wizard at divination, you may want to dive straight into Part II, but I encourage you to at least skim through the tools in Part I as you'll need them all later.

Part II: Building Your Ancestral Grimoire

Part II contains the juiciest bits on working through a solar year with your magical ancestors. You will then use the exercises, experiments, and insights to build a personal Ancestral Grimoire. This section is divided into twelve months, each highlighting a type of ancestral magic. You may choose to work with each month in real time or skip to the months that call to you. It's all good.

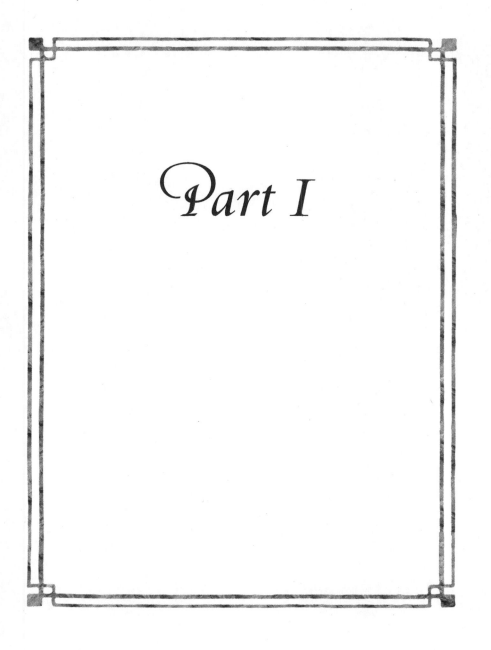

Part I

GETTING STARTED

And above all, watch with glittering eyes the whole world around you because the greatest secrets are always hidden in the most unlikely places. Those who don't believe in magic will never find it.

—ROALD DAHL

Settling into the Ancestral Realm

Things happen. You see a wisp out of the corner of your eye, you feel a strange tug when a song plays, what was lost has miraculously reappeared. As twilight turns to dusk and the sky fades to deep blue, something shifts in your vision, then fades. Again, just as dawn is peeking over the eastern horizon and the world is quiet, the feeling returns.

Depending on your background, you may attribute the odd feelings or the unexplained noise to the neighbors, fairy magic, happenstance, or a restless spirit seeking its home. But when the feeling persists—the sense of the unknown about to become known—you've traveled not to the Twilight Zone, but to the Ancestral Realm.

Perhaps you summoned the ancestors without realizing that your heartbeats were broadcasting out across time. There, they landed at the feet of the ones who love you. Although they live beyond your normal sensibilities, they can hear your wishes and feel your sorrows. They work for your happiness and help heal your pains. If you think life is a crapshoot, you don't know the tenth of the ancestral hands that pull you up, dust you off, and point the way forward.

One ancestor can be with you for a lifetime, another for just a moment. Ask for someone to show you the way out of darkness and they will hand you a blueprint no architect could even conceive.

Want to know your own *most potent form* of magic? Ask.

Your ancestors lived life across the spectrum of magic: the wise woman who knew which herb to prescribe, the bone-casting seer, the one who knew to place a fowl's feather inside a snakebite, the storyteller, and the story-saver. Regardless of the family in which you were raised, go far enough back in time and you'll find those ancestors who lived so close to nature that they instinctively knew how to work with energy.

And energy, my dear friend, is the key to magic.

In its simplest form, magic occurs when intent is combined with energy. Although it may not seem like "real" magic, it is. Imagine you're walking on a brisk fall afternoon. As you go, your mind is chewing over a work problem that feels unsolvable. You're hoping the walk will clear your mind (intent). As you walk, you feel drawn to reach down and pick up a red leaf (energy). Looking carefully at the veins running through the leaf, you have a flash of insight (intent + energy) on how to solve the problem (magic).

I know, this sounds supersimple, but it works. And if you merge your intent and energy with the energy of another object—the leaf, a candle, a tarot card, a coin, a tree, an ocean wave, a saint—"everyday magic" can become extraordinary magic.

The ancestors have been working with divination, omens, and natural energies for as long as we have records. The Aztecs threw dice, knucklebones were cast in ancient Asia Minor, priests communed with Apollo via the Oracle at Delphi, and in China the cracks in heated bone were interpreted as early as the 4th century BCE.

In the pages of this book, you're going to time travel across seas and continents. Your journey to ancestral magic will include both the common and the exotic. If you're ready for the adventure, your passport has been checked, and the gate is open.

Now We Begin

If you had a diary when you were eight years old, you may have written about your latest crush, your fight with your bestie, or the restrictions mom or dad put on your online time.

You may still keep a diary of sorts, but yours might be in the form of a grimoire (grim-wohr)—or a Book of Shadows. This is where you'll detail your personal magical experiences throughout this journey.

If you're already tracking the cycles of the moon or drawing a daily tarot card, then you have a journal started. But even if you do, I'm going to ask you to create a new one: an Ancestral Book of Shadows. This is where you'll save the magical knowledge that relates directly to your lineage.

Use your book to track your journey. Write down meaningful dreams, the ancestors you meet, ancestral magic tarot or oracle spreads, pendulum practices, casting divinations, and even encounters with spirits, angels, or other nonhuman entities. Each person's book will be as unique as each person's lineage.

And yes, even if you're adopted, you can still work with your ancestors. In fact, this is one impactful way to get to know them.

Your ancestors are plentiful. Some of them can't wait to work with you; others have a separate path to walk in the afterlife. And of those millions on the other side, there are both the magical and the nonmagical. It's here where I need to pause and say: What we call magic *could* have been magic to your ancestors, or it could have just been how they did life. Did my grandmother's knowledge of folk medicine make her magical? While she would say no, I would say yes. Were those who successfully prayed for rain or watched the animals for signs of an early snow magical? Again, I would say yes.

Ancestral lives—especially those of hundreds or even thousands of years ago—are so different from ours. But regardless of circumstances, we face similar challenges. True, your predator may be an overly friendly coworker while theirs was a snow leopard. You found the courage to report inappropriate behavior to HR while they became adept at spear throwing. But both of you worked from an innate understanding of the surrounding energy.

What do you say you try to learn at least a little of what they knew?

If you follow along with the twelve months of exercises in Part II of this book, you'll tap into the wisdom and experience of twelve of your ancestors. Some were powerful magicians; others practiced everyday magic. All have something to share with you. As each month turns into the next, you will amass a wealth of wisdom designed to enrich your life. You will find the magic that runs through your family lines.

Creating Your Ancestral Book of Shadows

Your book can be divided into whatever form you like—since it's yours. The Part II exercises are divided into a solar calendar of twelve months. However, if you already work with seasonal energies or the eight sabbats on the Wheel of the Year that's fine too.

Although your ancestors didn't name the thing we call the Wheel of the Year, they followed it because they followed the seasons. Go back a few hundred years and much of everyday life was based on Earth changes seen around the solstices and equinoxes. The Wheel of the Year is a convenient calendar for us that marks the turning of the Earth on its axis, a motion that creates the seasons.

You're going to learn how to tap into the energy of the changing seasons, then use that energy to work with and shift your own inner landscape.

If you live in a small town or rural area, your approach to ancestral work through the year may be different from an urban dweller like me. Your ancestors may guide you to conversations with a fox or hedgehog while mine might be with a neighborhood cat or squirrel. Though our paths will diverge, the work we do together will be the same. We are ancestor hunter-gatherers.

As you go through each month, season, or sabbat, you will build a catalog of magical knowledge that is *personal to you and no one else*. The more you learn, the stronger a connection you will build to your own lineage. Every family line has its own form of magic, and you will discover yours.

In Your Backpack

1. Of course, you'll need a blank book—a beautiful one or a rustic one or a kitschy one. It's your ancestors, so it's your choice. You can divide the book any way you like, although my divisions in Part II are in calendar months.

2. Pens and colored pencils. You may want to sketch your nature journeys or the friends you meet along the way.

3. Glue. For those moments when you find a photo or magazine article that feels like it should be included.

4. At least one tarot deck—two are preferable, more even better. Chapter 5 is crammed with information on choosing a deck, but for right now pick one you're comfortable with. If the ancestors don't like it, they'll let you know. How? By losing cards, making your shuffles fly all over the room, or spilling your drink on a deck they don't like! If you're clairaudient, you may easily hear their preference.

   John B., in working through the exercises in my previous book, *Ancestral Tarot*, wrote me saying:

   These ancestors are fussy. Very specific about the deck I use for them! I was using the DruidCraft, but my guides directed me to use The Wildwood Tarot. My mother's Italians wanted something more European, so they agreed to a Marseille deck . . . My dad's mother's family insisted on something more British and refined (with real Royals). They settled on the RWS [Rider-Waite-Smith].

5. Cool stuff to decorate your pages; think washi tape, animal stickies, labels, pictures of the family or family cemeteries . . . Once you begin, you'll figure it out.

6. One or two oracle decks

7. A pendulum—I'll show you how to DIY one.

8. A pendulum board—ditto on the DIY.

9. Index cards for creating supplementary cards

10. Things to cast (wooden disks, charms, stones)

You Have to Start Somewhere

One of the first questions I'm asked is how to begin working with the ancestors—how to make that first connection. There's an inner journey that I'll suggest in Chapter 4, but for right now, get out your tarot deck and separate it into three piles: Major Arcana, the Court cards, and finally the remainder of the Minor Arcana. In fact, if you own multiple decks you may want to keep one of them separated like this as you work through this book.

A standard tarot deck actually consists of two different types of cards. The Major Arcana consists of twenty-two named cards, such as Death, Judgement, the Moon, or the Empress. The Minor Arcana consist of fifty-six cards, divided into four suits. Similarly to standard playing cards, each suit contains cards numbered from 1 to 10. Sixteen of these fifty-six cards are known as the Court Cards, as they depict members of a royal court: kings, queens, knights, and pages.

This exercise is just a tiny toe-dip into ancestral waters.

As with all ancestral work, please ask that your ancestors keep watch over you and protect you from any entity with a lower vibration than yours or that does not have your highest good at heart.

Now, set an intention.

An *intention* is a clearly focused goal and an integral part of a strong ancestral magical foundation. Pulling cards without a clear intention won't give you the desired outcome because you didn't identify what you are looking for. Setting an intention will open clear channels of energy and make sure your message is received.

An example of an intention would be "I invite an ancestor who can help with my health issues," or "I would like to speak with an ancestor who can help with letting go of the grief around my ex."

Once you have a clear intention, shuffle the sixteen Court cards. When you feel the energy is right, fan the cards out facedown. Move your left hand over the cards and pause when you feel a tingling in your palm as it passes over one of the cards. Turn that card faceup. This is a first look at an ancestor.

Because Court cards are often the most challenging for tarot readers— and the ones you'll be using throughout the book to identify particular ancestors—I've included the most important things you need to know about them in Chapter 2.

Next, draw a card from the Major Arcana. This card represents the most important energy your ancestor can share with you. Since you're going to be meeting several magical ancestors, knowing the energy that they worked and now share with you is damned important.

Let me share an example of this in my own work. I asked for the ancestor who could balance unstable or ill-distributed energy. My ancestor appeared as the Knight of Cups. This is the Knight who is in love with love. Plus, he's kinder than kind. I asked for the energy this ancestor used to create balance and one he would share with me. I drew the Magician. This is the Major Arcana card that guides us to match our energy with that which we desire. Then, magic happens.

Your turn. Once you've drawn your ancestor (Court card), draw a Major Arcana for their magical energy—the one they want to share with you.

Make sure you write this down and that you understand the message before moving forward as you'll be working with this ancestor in Chapter 2.

MEET THE ANCESTORS

ourt cards—the Royals—live at the heart of the Ancestral Tarot practice since we use them to identify ancestral personalities. Through these cards, we can get a glimpse of the face an ancestor is showing us. (They may have shown another face to the world, however.)

Courts 101

Before diving in deeper, let's deal with the basics. There are four Court cards or royals for each of the four tarot suits of Wands, Cups, Swords, and Pentacles, meaning there are sixteen in all. They are typically called Page, Knight, Queen, and King. However, depending on the deck that you use, they may have other names or titles instead, such as:

- ∴ Princess, Prince, Queen, King (as in *The DruidCraft Tarot*)
- ∴ Child, Explorer, Guardian, Elder (as in the *Gaian Tarot*)
- ∴ Daughter, Son, Mother, Father (as in the *Vision Quest Tarot*)

Historically, physical characteristics, gender, and age were assigned to the Court cards. For example, the Queen of Cups was identified as a middle-aged woman with blond hair and blue eyes. But in our world of gender fluidity, such designations are archaic. The King of Pentacles could easily be a female head of household. And when it comes to age, the traditional assignments just don't work. I've seen adults who act like children and children who act like adults. Haven't you?

Just be aware of your own expectations when you see a Court card. For example, I've often drawn a Page for someone I know died as a young adult, even though the card looks like a child. When it comes to the ancestors, understanding personality is much more important than getting hung up on someone's age.

The following charts contain the least you need to know about the members of the Courts—and will be sufficient for the purposes of this book. You'll come to know them better through your own interactions with them in the exercises to come.

Each rank acts a certain way, and that way is defined by the element of the suit.

Ranks

PAGE	KNIGHT	QUEEN	KING
Learners, youthful enthusiasm	Questers, action-oriented	Nurturers, attendants	Rule-makers, rule-enforcers

Elements

WANDS	CUPS	SWORDS	PENTACLES
Fire	Water	Air	Earth
Passionate	Emotional	Thinker	Practical

Looking at the Page of Wands, you know that this ancestor went about his life with youthful enthusiasm. But if you add in the element (Wands/Fire), you'll gain a secondary layer to help understand his personality. From the Elements chart, you know that this Page is full of Fire energy—passion, perhaps lacking in patience. He has enthusiasm about whatever he's doing. For me it says this person, while incarnate, got in trouble more than once due to impulsivity. The Page of Swords, however, would have taken a thoughtful approach to new experiences. (No leaping before looking!)

Important to remember: Drawing a Court card to represent an ancestor is only going to show you one facet of their personality. That facet is the one to which you will most easily relate.

The Shadow Side of the Royals

Court cards can also show you a side of an ancestor that perhaps you didn't expect.

Here's the deal: A reversed Royal shows the shadow side of their personality. One of my aunts was the Queen of Swords (honest and straightforward), but when reversed, her shadow side could be cold and distant. Just as we show two sides to the world of our inner self and outer mask, we also can be the reverse of both.

Let me give you another example.

Imagine that you wear the outer mask of the Queen of Swords and the inner self of the Queen of Cups. What are they reversed? Well, the Queen of Swords (as you just saw) can be cold and cutting, while the Queen of Cups can be guilt-ridden and so empathetic that she sacrifices her own well-being.

Further in the book, as you work with the ancestors, you'll be uncovering several facets of a single ancestor, and this will help you understand how they managed to maintain their magical self out in the big, bad world.

Although I'm going to go through each of the Court cards, here's a handy cheat sheet. I want to emphasize, though, that the more you work with the ancestors, the more keywords you can fill in. And all this goes in your grimoire.

COURT CARD	UPRIGHT	REVERSED	NOTES
Page of Pentacles	Studious	Bored	
Page of Wands	Impulsive	Childish	
Page of Swords	Curious	Cutting	
Page of Cups	Loving	Supersensitive	
Knight of Pentacles	Methodical	Too cautious	
Knight of Wands	Risk-taker	Too incautious	
Knight of Swords	Idea-seeker	Abrupt	
Knight of Cups	Love-seeker	Starry-eyed	
Queen of Pentacles	Physical nurturer	Smothering	
Queen of Wands	Intuitive	Impatient	
Queen of Swords	Truth-teller	Cold	
Queen of Cups	Emotional nurturer	Suffocating	
King of Pentacles	Solid	Selfish	
King of Wands	Visionary	Smug	
King of Swords	Precise	Dismissive	
King of Cups	Helpful guidance	Too emotional	

Let's talk a little more about the shadow side. What, exactly, does that mean? A shadow side is an underexpressed part of who you are. It could be a trait that you don't like or one that you don't want to show the world. It's the one that would embarrass you if anyone knew about it. The shadow side is the one you keep hidden.

If you draw an ancestral card reversed, the question to ask is, *why are you being shown a shadow side?* For me, it's a warning of what could happen if I fall off the path. For you, it could be something different.

Let me give you one more example. The King of Cups is often depicted as a jolly fellow who loves to have fun, maybe eat and drink too much, and be everybody's friend. He'll welcome you over to watch a football game and lay out the best food ever. (I'm sure pizza is involved.) At his core, it's possible that what he wants most in life is to be loved and admired. So what's his shadow side? He doesn't have good boundaries because if he says no, it's possible someone won't love him anymore. Does that make sense?

If you're struggling with boundaries, it wouldn't be surprising if the reversed King of Cups showed up . . .

Or what about a reversed Page, regardless of suit? How would you interpret an adult who appears as a Page? It's possible that they approached life in a childish way or, when they were angry, they acted out. Think about the best and worst traits of a child and you'll have some idea about adults who appear as upright or reversed Pages.

But that's enough of examples. Let's go through all sixteen of the Court cards in more detail. As you read along, try to imagine someone you know—whether family, friends, or coworkers—that fits the description. Once you have a real person in your mind, it's going to be simple for you to interpret the Courts.

Meet the Royals

Just for ease of reading, I'll use the pronouns that fit the cards, but in Chapter 5 I'll show you an effortless way to discover gender along with a few other useful tricks.

The Kings

The Kings are the masters of their suits. They've learned the lessons of youth, have made mistakes, and learned hard lessons. The Kings seen in a tarot deck like the Rider-Waite-Smith are from an era when a king had to be a warrior. You may or may not remember that Richard III lost his kingdom when he was killed on the battlefield. So much for hereditary kingships.

KING OF WANDS

This is the Fire King, associated with the astrological sign of Leo. He is also associated with spring, the time of year when seedlings pop up through the snow and trees begin to releaf. Spring is dynamic, just like the King of Wands.

He is a visionary, a leader, and an expert at implementing the things for which he has a passion. He is the most freethinking of the Kings, action-oriented, and has no problems thinking or operating outside the box.

If you know any Leos, you'll know that when they're in a good place, they're charming as hell. They're the person everyone wants to be around. Like the Sun, they shine so brilliantly we all want to bask in their glow. King Leo loves starting new things, is action-oriented, and has little patience for anything or anyone getting in his way. He can be an effective leader because he is inspirational.

Shadow Side: Who is this person when the card is drawn reversed (upside down)? King Leo is ultrasensitive to criticism, but what wounds him even more than criticism is being ignored. Let him shine and he's golden. Ignore him and you'll see the destructive element of Fire.

KING OF CUPS

This is the King of Summer and associated with the watery sign of Scorpio. Okay, if you know any Scorpios, right now you may be saying, "Oh, no!" Scorpios get a bad rap because they're intense. But think about it: when you're in love, aren't you displaying the most intense behavior ever?

King Love has learned how to control his feelings a little bit better than the Queen. He is just as empathetic, but where the Queen's empathy will lead toward taking care of you, it's more in the King's nature to give you a referral to his favorite massage therapist or Reiki practitioner.

This is the touchy-feely King. He loves deeply, is incredibly creative, and is drawn to beauty. Because he is a watery king, his emotions can be fluid. He can love you intensely today, but tomorrow be lukewarm. This fluidity is how he remains in balance. If you think about going around all the time in a state of intense emotions, you'll have an idea of why this King must ratchet back a little to keep balanced.

Shadow Side: So what could be the shadow side of the King of Cups? He could overly indulge in the things he loves, whether that is women, alcohol, or his next great enterprise. Ignoring his head warnings, he can get into deep shit when he lets his emotions control his behavior. If you turn him down as a lover, he could turn into a stalker.

KING OF SWORDS

This is the Air King. His astrological association is Aquarius, and his season is fall. King Air is the master of the mind. He is visionary, focused, and has ideas that are far-out. His ideas are a year or two ahead of the rest of us; he is always ahead of his time. Do you know any Aquarians? If so, you know that their mind is going 100 mph and they have their fingers in ten fires all at the same time. They are an idea machine.

This is the guy you want going over your latest contract or vetting a new plumber. He is mentally swift, quickly makes decisions, knows how to cut through red tape, and—like his counterpart, the Queen—prides himself on his honesty.

Shadow Side: The shadow side of this Aquarian King is his natural ability to hurt your feelings without ever knowing it. He is so into his mental world that anything warm and fuzzy and material simply doesn't exist. In fact, the world outside of his own thoughts is foreign to him. If you want to have a good relationship with this King, talk to him in the language of ideas, not the language of feelings.

Oh, did I forget to mention? Never play poker with this guy. Trust me, he's the one who invented the term *poker face*.

KING OF PENTACLES

Here we find the Earth King, associated with the earthiest of Earth signs: Taurus. His is the realm of winter. If you look at the King of Pentacles in almost every deck, he's surrounded by opulence. Typically, you'll see flourishing plants or grape clusters around him. He also wears rich robes of gold, red, or purple. Each of his physical needs is met. He is much like the Emperor (Major Arcana 4) in that he rules a kingdom in which everyone is well taken care of. Think about the Taureans in your life. They are the Earth sign most concerned with physical security: home, money, possessions.

He is good with money, land, the harvest, bank books, and family. He is not beyond having a fun time, but he is the one who is most apt to tell you how to manage your finances or where to get a better school loan.

Shadow Side: Can you guess what the Winter King's shadow side might be? This king can be so attached to his stuff that it's almost impossible to move him off the dime. He simply won't let go, even if holding on is destroying him and/or his family. He can also at his worst spend money to get back at someone—even if it means going into debt. If you anger the shadow side of this King, he can slice you out of his life as though he were the King of Swords.

The Queens

| QUEEN of WANDS | QUEEN of CUPS | QUEEN of SWORDS | QUEEN of PENTACLES |

The Queens in the Royal Court are a fascinating bunch. They are a compilation of all the traits ascribed to women. They could be a lover, mother, sister, aunt, niece, granny, or mother-in-law. They can house you, feed you, inspire you, and tell you the truths that you really don't want to hear. As with the Kings, each Queen is associated with an element, a season, and a suit.

QUEEN OF WANDS

The Spring Queen is the Fire Queen, associated with Aries—that ram-headed go-getter. She is a person of action, impulse, and vibrancy. Upright, she is intuitive, psychic, energized, and in motion. Her kingdom is the kingdom of Fire, so she knows how to initiate as well as how to keep a spark blazing.

This is the intuitive Queen. She tempers her impulsivity with wisdom and intuition. She knows exactly when to step in to help and exactly when to remain on the sidelines. She can light a fire under you if she sees you being lazy and can prod you into action if she thinks you need to get off your butt. She is charismatic and charming, with lots of friends who adore her. Good luck to anyone who can convince her to be their partner as she is the most independent of the Queens.

Shadow Side: This reversed Queen can be so focused on whatever she's doing that she may forget to pick the kids up at school. She can also get scorched herself, because her impulsivity can lead her into dangerous or ill-advised situations. At her worst, she can burn you.

QUEEN OF CUPS

This is the Queen of Summer, ruled by the zodiac sign of watery Cancer. This alone should give you a clue about her personality. She is emotional and talks a lot in terms of how she feels, rather than what she thinks. She will give you a big hug and a shoulder to cry on when you're blue because she knows what it's like to have big feelings. She is also intuitive, but not in the same way as the Queen of Wands. For this Queen, her intuition is more about being clairsentient—she can feel what you feel.

She is compassionate and empathetic and will give you an aspirin when you're sick, balloons and confetti for your special days, and send you sweet love notes. She is a caretaker, lover, and cheerleader, with an unending amount of affection.

Shadow Side: You've heard the term *smother mother?* That's the Queen of Cups. She can be indulgent to the nth degree. She lacks boundaries and can be so overly sensitive that you must watch what you say around her. Unlike the King of Cups, she won't keep trying to change your mind, but she will let you know how very, very hurt she is. That way you can feel guilty.

QUEEN OF SWORDS

I must admit this is my favorite Queen. She arrives in fall. You will often see birds and butterflies on her card as they are both creatures of Air. She is associated with Libra—you know, the one with the scales. My favorite thing about Madam Sword is that she tells the truth. She is intelligent, has lots of ideas, and uses her brain to get what she wants. However, unlike the

Aquarian King of Swords, she's not invested in the most brilliant invention of the century; her ideas go much more toward enjoying her world of knowledge. She will google anything and everything.

She is smart, aggressive, honest, edgy, and straightforward. If you don't want to hear the truth, don't ask. She does not suffer fools, is not warm and fuzzy, and has no dearth of opinions. This Queen is a wonderful confidante, even though she can be intimidating. But once you gain her trust, you can tell her anything and have absolute faith that she will never betray your confidence.

Shadow Side: Oh, man, I wish she didn't have one. But she does. She can be cutting—as sharp as a surgeon's scalpel, especially if you come to her with sloppy thinking. Don't bring an idea to her that isn't well thought out. She has no tolerance for stupidity or ignorance. Want to get along with her? Bring your A game.

QUEEN OF PENTACLES

The beautiful Queen of Earth lives in the astrological sign of Capricorn. If you know Caps, you know they're superorganized. You're not going to walk into a clutter-fest when you visit this Queen. She won't give you the shoulder to cry on like the Queen of Cups, but she will feed you homemade bread and soup. She is down-to-earth, just as you'd suppose her to be. Because of that Capricorn nature, she can be a successful entrepreneur.

Think of the epitome of an earthy person (remember, your male ancestor may show up as a Queen) and what adjectives come to mind? Kind, practical, grounded, home lovers, animal lovers, good with material things. In the tarot this is the Queen who will make up the spare bedroom and fix your favorite cake for your birthday. But don't be fooled by her feminine qualities; she can be just as adept at plowing a field or wielding a hammer (think Brigid).

Shadow Side: Well, I must admit this Queen can make you nuts picking up your coffee cup while you're still drinking, just to make sure it gets into the sink. She's also a great money-minder but can be too cautious when it comes to buying something she really wants; better to save it just in case. For me, the shadow side of this Queen is her inability to make a quick decision. If you really need her to say yes or no right now, you're in for a long wait.

The Knights

KNIGHT OF SWORDS   KNIGHT OF PENTACLES

Something that all four Knights share is that they're on a quest. If you look at all the RWS Knights you'll see that they wear full armor. In the *Bone-stone & Earthflesh* the Knights have no armor, and in fact are scantily clad. Why do you think that is?

THE KNIGHT OF WANDS

In some decks, this guy rides a horse with a flaming mane and tail, which tells you something about him. He's impulsive—just like the others of his suit—but a little more dangerous because he's running around with a club. He is associated with Sagittarius (the Centaur) and the element of Fire. He gets anxious if you make him sit still (can you imagine being his teacher?) and is in his element when on the move. What's he looking for? Adventure, as he is a natural explorer.

If you draw this card as an ancestor, you're dealing with someone who is a bit less impulsive than the Page, but not by a lot. He is the one who needs to be in action or in movement. The most painful torture for this

Knight is boredom. He can't really settle down into learning something like the Knight of Pentacles does, nor does he do a deep dive into esoteric knowledge like Swords. Instead, he dips in and out of anything that catches his eye.

Shadow Side: Like the King and Queen of Wands, this Knight can behave horribly if you make him wait for anything. If you told him he needed a passport to get into France, he's the one most likely to tear up the paperwork and make a run for it through the border crossing. His shadowy curse is laziness. Instead of feeding the internal fire, he throws water on it.

KNIGHT OF CUPS

This Piscean Knight lives in a world of dreamy dreams. He's on the quest for love and beauty. He romanticizes whatever or whomever he's in love with in the moment. He loves beauty in all of its forms and is apt to ascribe some divine meaning to the mundane. He is so convinced that he's found his perfect mate, perfect job, or perfect home that he'll have you convinced too. I think he's the purest of the Knights, the one who can truly envision a perfect world, and, because of that, he's the one most easily disappointed.

Like the Page, this Knight is an ancestor who longed for true love. In fact, he may have gone through several relationships or even marriages seeking that "perfect" mate. Don't be surprised when you do a family tree to find the Knight of Cups married to a Pentacle. That's because the earthiness of Pentacles grounds the watery Cups. Unfortunately, this Knight may have trouble finding satisfaction in life unless he genuinely loves what he's doing.

Shadow Side: The reversed Knight of Cups can be the dandy, the person who loves being in love. He can be a brooder if his true love doesn't love him back, and he can try a lot of silly—but in his mind romantic—ways to win them back. He has difficulty understanding that his love just isn't that into him. Because of his ultra-water nature, he does better when guided by a more earthy helper/partner/mentor.

KNIGHT OF SWORDS

This Knight is on a quest to ingest all the knowledge in the world. Bored? Teach yourself calculus. Don't know what to do with yourself on summer vacation? Learn Scottish Gaelic (looking at you Alison Cross). He is an Air Knight and lives in the realm of Gemini. Mental gymnastics are his favorite pastimes, and cramming in as much information as possible in as short a time as possible is his idea of heaven.

This Knight has moved from checkers to 3D chess. He loves chasing innovative ideas, making plans, changing plans, exploring new theories, and in the process being one of those people who knows many things about many topics. He is a sponge when it comes to absorbing knowledge and information.

Shadow Side: Because of his connection to Gemini, the Knight of Swords can be easily distracted, going in one direction after another, or endlessly chasing ideas. Because he has not attained the maturity of the Queen or King of Swords, he can doubt his ideas, which means he can doubt himself.

KNIGHT OF PENTACLES

This earthy Knight is associated with my own sun sign of Virgo. He loves his home and his friends, is unbelievably loyal, and keeps everyone in order. Of all the Knights, he is the only one who is not in motion. He sits on his big-ass horse, looking out over his land. He's patient, takes things as they come, and is practical in his approach to life, work, and love.

Like the Page, he is devoted to learning, but now he's branched out from books to hands-on learning. I remember a visit to my uncle's farm where at the end of each row of corn there was a sign showing what had been used on the corn (I suspect fertilizer or pesticide). I can see this Knight taking great pleasure in keeping a spreadsheet of those rows of corn and how well they grow. Look for an ancestor who did things one at a time, slowly, methodically.

Shadow Side: This Knight can be so slow he'll drive you nuts. If he's interested in something, he'll research it until he's attained as much knowledge as a college professor. So what if you don't want to know about the love letters between John and Abigail Adams? He's going to tell you about them anyway. When it comes to his shadow side, unless you know him quite well you may never see it as he keeps his emotions under a tight rein.

The Pages

The Pages can be children or also young adults, so don't be fooled when a Page appears. Historically, Pages are the young people sent to a castle to work as a helper to a knight—a squire. The easiest way to think about Pages is that they represent a person who is in the initial stages of learning the craft of their suit.

PAGE OF WANDS

The Fire Page is associated with all the Fire signs: Aries, Leo, and Sagittarius. She—like the Courts we've met before—is impulsive. This is a young person who is on the move but because of her inexperience may not have a clear focus. She wants to *go* but isn't sure where. A trickster, this Page is learning how to play with—and control—fire. She will do well when her high energy can be focused in a positive direction.

This truly is a firecracker of a personality: impulsive, mischievous, risk-taking, learning by doing rather than reading. This Page will jump in the deep end of a swimming pool before learning to swim, confident in her ability to get to the side of the pool.

Shadow Side: This is the kid who was always in trouble in school. A prankster or class clown, the Page of Wands can end up in trouble so often she can give up on herself. She talks before she thinks; she leaps before she looks.

PAGE OF CUPS

This Page has parts of all three Water signs: Cancer, Scorpio, Pisces. She is a person who needs to be guided into pursuits that feed her sense of purpose through art, music, or drama. She is intuitive, easily noticing other people's feelings, but sometimes, because she is inexperienced, she misunderstands subtle emotional cues from others. She is at home in the water and more comfortable around those who support her dreams.

The Page of Cups is very Piscean in nature: artistic, creative, dreamy, not well-grounded, seeming to always be searching for the *ideal*, whether it is the ideal project, partner, job, school, diet, journal, chair—you name it. These Pages have an innate sense of what they're seeking. Don't try to substitute an imitation. It won't work and will just annoy them.

Shadow Side: Like others who represent the element of Water, this Page can have her feelings easily hurt. She can withdraw if she senses criticism or hide away both physically and emotionally if she's not surrounded by loving family or friends. Encourage and support her dreams and you'll help guide a loving soul.

PAGE OF SWORDS

The Page of Air is associated with Gemini, Libra, and Aquarius. She is the smartest kid in the class, although not the typical nerd. She can be just as good at softball as she is at chess. (That's because she understands the physics behind a baseball.) She has an insatiable curiosity and will tackle multiple subjects across multiple genres—all because they have something that interests her. She may not understand all that she reads, but she reads it anyway. Unlike the Knight of Swords, she can't play 3D chess, but she can play an unbeatable game of checkers.

This person is at the beginning of a lifetime of study, which may vary across interests and industries, from engineering to video games or playing table tennis.

Shadow Side: The Page of Air is such a know-it-all that she doesn't ask for help or guidance. She may be smarter than anyone in school, but that doesn't mean she knows what she's doing. You've heard about kids who are constantly asking you why. That is the Page of Swords.

PAGE OF PENTACLES

Every teacher's favorite student, the Page of Pentacles loves learning for the sake of learning. She is studious, quiet, rarely gets into trouble, and can get lost in the distant past or the far future, depending on what book she's reading at the time. Like the Knight of this suit, she loves new ideas, but where the Knight can be focused, the Page is the one who can start an internet search for "tennis racquets" and four hours later be deep down a rabbit hole reading about alien abductions.

The Page of Pentacles is going to be someone in Spirit who was serious. They approached their life as an opportunity to gain experience, whether it was in the ABCs or advanced mathematics or chemical engineering. They found comfort and reassurance in what they could find in previously written knowledge.

Shadow Side: This Page is so comfortable immersed in a world of books and computers that she can be a loner, making few good friends. Although an earthy Page who really loves nature, she can get lost in research and forget to go outside. Or forget that she promised to meet you for coffee after class.

Ask for an Ancestor

One of the most valuable things you can do with the ancestors is to call in one who can help with a specific situation. You can do this a couple of ways: Ask for an ancestor who was successful in dealing with whatever problem you have. Or ask for one who was *not* successful, so that they can tell you where they went off the rails.

Before going any further, pull out the Court card for the ancestor you met in Chapter 1. This is just for practice, so trust your intuition. Place that Court card in position 2 in the spread here. Next, draw four cards from the entire deck.

The cards in this spread will tell you the following:

1. What was one of your magical skills? (They may have had more than one.)

2. The ancestor you've already drawn (Court card).

3, 4, 5. What can you teach me about your magic?

Let's explore the process with a concrete example of the cards I pulled.

Looking at the Eight of Swords, the magic I can imagine is one of escape using the power of the mind. I can see this ancestor seemingly cornered but using his masterful manipulation of illusion to exit the situation. But what of the other three cards? They are all Wands, all action. So, while this Knight (your ancestor) may be a little slow, he does know what he's seeking. He manifests action based on his desires.

Is this making sense for you? If so, read on. If not, well read on then too, as we look at how to interpret the tarot from an ancestral perspective.

Next

Make notes about your interpretation of each of the sixteen Court cards. Then pick someone you know that fits the personality of each card. If you can't think of someone you know personally, see if there's a celebrity fit.

Bonus points if you can match a friend, teacher, coworker, or family member who walks on the shadow side of each of the Court cards.

SEASONS, MONTHS, AND SABBATS

First, Science

I read the other day that time is one of the most measured things in our world. The US Naval Observatory (USNO) in Washington, DC, houses the world's most accurate timepiece: the Master Clock. That's what keeps the time on your computer accurate and gets you across town using GPS.

Since you're going to be working through twelve months, let's talk just a bit about time and how to configure your grimoire.

The Seasons

The twelve-month Western calendar is divided into four seasons: spring, summer, autumn, and winter.

Weather changes noticeably from season to season unless you live in a place where seasonal changes are subtle, such as Southern California. As the seasons change, so does the quality of light. Wherever you live, working with the seasons is about perceiving the shift in energy, no matter how small it may appear.

Depending on where you are located, seasons may be extreme. I remember my college days in the Midwest, sitting at a desk toward the end of the dreariest of winters. I looked out my window, and there, pushing up through the mud and snow, was a shoot of green. I can't describe how seeing that bit of green made me feel; the closest I can come is to say it felt like the world was waking up.

And now, because I'm a geek, please allow me a tiny bit of science about the seasons.

We Live on a Lopsided Orange

Unlike a top, Earth does not rotate on a vertical axis. Instead, we tilt. That means as we travel around the sun, different parts of our tilt are pointed at the sun. When the North Pole tilts toward the sun, it's summer in the Northern Hemisphere. When the South Pole tilts toward the sun, it's summer in the Southern Hemisphere.

In March (spring equinox) and September (fall equinox) the sun shines equally on both the Northern and Southern Hemispheres.

Last point: we don't orbit the sun in a perfect circle either; instead, we whirl through space in a kind of oval trajectory. That means sometimes we're closer to the sun than at other times. However, the distance does not determine seasons. In fact, we're closest to the sun in January and furthest in July. Weird, huh?

The Equinoxes

Spring begins when the sun crosses the equator, moving from the Southern to the Northern Hemisphere, and the North Pole begins to point toward the sun. Conversely, fall begins when the sun crosses the equator from the Northern Hemisphere to the Southern, and the South Pole begins to point toward the sun.

Although the dates may change slightly, the spring equinox is near March 20 and the fall equinox near September 22. The equinox dates are just reversed in the Southern Hemisphere.

The Solstices

The word *solstice* comes from the Latin *sol* ("sun") and *sistere* ("to stand still"). The reason the ancients thought that time was standing still was that on these two days the shadow cast by a sundial moved very little.

Do you remember when I said that our axis tilts? Well, the dates of the maximum tilt correspond to the summer and winter solstices. Summer's is near June 21, and winter's near December 21. In the Southern Hemisphere, the dates are reversed.

Isn't it wonderful that our ancestors didn't have to know all this science to understand when a season changed? Sometimes all it took was realizing that when the sun rose over a specific peak, there was a discernible shift in the energy.

As you work with the ancestors through the three months of each season, think about how life two hundred years ago would have revolved around the seasons. Do a little research and see what your knowledge and intuition tell you. Also, how is your own life impacted by the seasons?

The Months

Our calendar has gone through more than one change over the centuries. The current Western calendar is known as the Gregorian calendar, named after Pope Gregory XIII in 1582, replacing the earlier Julian calendar.

Great Britain and its colonies, including what would become the United States, adopted the Gregorian calendar in 1752; other countries, such as Russia, did so even later. George Washington, for example, was born on February 11, 1731, according to the Julian calendar, but to make this correspond with the modern Gregorian calendar, we must add one year and eleven days—making his birthday February 22, 1732. While this is massively confusing, calendar date converters are easily found online.

The Sabbats

The Neo-Pagan festivals known as sabbats are associated with the changing of the seasons. The word *sabbat* derives from the Latin *sabbatum* or "sabbath." When you hear the phrase "Wheel of the Year," the reference is to the eight sabbats, which are often visualized as forming a wheel.

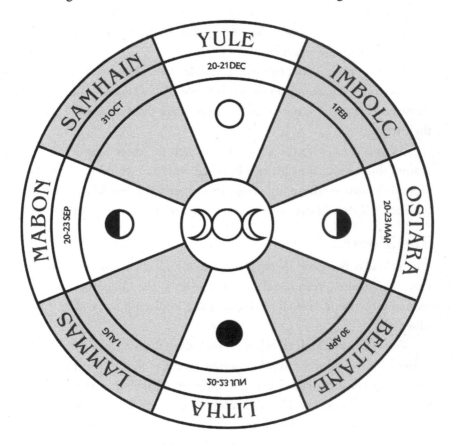

Equinox and Solstice Sabbats

Dates are approximate.

OSTARA	LITHA	MABON	YULE
Spring Equinox	Summer Solstice	Fall Equinox	Winter Solstice
March 19–21 Northern Hemisphere	June 20–22 Northern Hemisphere	September 21–24 Northern Hemisphere	December 21 Northern Hemisphere
September 21–24 Southern Hemisphere	December 21 Southern Hemisphere	March 19–21 Southern Hemisphere	June 20–22 Southern Hemisphere
Resurgence, Fertility	Sun, Celebration	Second Harvest, Rest	Light in Darkness, Rebirth

Cross-Quarter Sabbats

These are the midpoints of each of the four seasons.

IMBOLC	BELTANE	LAMMAS	SAMHAIN
Between winter solstice and spring equinox	Between spring equinox and summer solstice	Between summer solstice and fall equinox	Between fall equinox and winter solstice
February 1–2 Northern Hemisphere	May 1 Northern Hemisphere	August 1–2 Northern Hemisphere	October 31 Northern Hemisphere
August 1–2 Southern Hemisphere	October 31 Southern Hemisphere	February 1–2 Southern Hemisphere	May 1 Southern Hemisphere
Creativity, Renewal	Sexuality, Passion	Harvest, Abundance	Feast of the Dead, Ancestors, Introspection

If you want to work with ancestors in each of the sabbats, you'll find additional information and new spreads for each in Appendix C.

It's your decision about how to configure your grimoire. If you don't know which is best for your ancestral magic work—months or the Wheel of the Year—draw a card for each. I'm certain you'll get a quick and easy-to-interpret answer. Mine was the Nine of Cups—months, without a doubt.

THE LAND OF TAROT

Meeting the Seventy-Eight

In Chapter 2 we started associating the tarot Court cards with ancestral personalities, but I want to give you one more layer to use when working with not only the Courts, but the whole deck. This is a visualization that will take you to the Land of Tarot. There, you can gain insights on a different level than you will get with a reading. This is a short chapter, so stay with me, even if you're not keen on using visualization.

During this process you'll enter your own inner landscape and create a place to connect with the people who live in the tarot deck. Here, the people will be walking around, talking with each other and with you. This visualization makes it easy to understand everyone as living people and not just a character on a card.

The Land of Tarot that you will create via visualization will never be like anyone else's. This is the gateway through which you can meet every single person in a deck, chat with them, and really learn who they are at their core. To get there, all it takes is a little visualization.

Here's How

I suggest reading through this process before doing it. That way you won't have to stop mid-visualization to read what to do next.

Find a quiet spot where you won't be disturbed. Turn off any device that may beep, chirp, or ring. Next, allow yourself to relax. Close your eyes, drop your shoulders, let a few big breaths of air whoosh out through your mouth.

Next, take two to three deep breaths down into your belly. Breathe in through your nose and out through your mouth. Do this deep breathing as long as it takes to relax your body and allow your mind to wander freely.

Once you are settled, picture walking through a rainbow of energy going from red to orange to yellow; then yellow to green, blue, indigo, violet, and finally white. When you step out of the white energy and open your inner eyes, you'll be in the Land of Tarot.

What you envision there may be a meadow, a waterfall, outer space, near a dragon, within a castle, or even under the sea. Whatever you envision, it is perfect. You may meet the Fool, a unicorn, or a talking boulder. As you wander through the landscape, it's possible a guide will approach you. Or you could randomly meet a tarot character. Give yourself permission to walk, fly, or flutter across the land, stopping when you see someone you want to meet.

Over time and many trips there, you may find the landscape changing or the people moving in and out. Trust whom you meet; be open to what you hear. You can ask for a certain person to come forward; they may or they may not. This is a land of surprises.

For me, the Land of Tarot begins with jumping off a cliff with the Fool. I never know exactly where I'll land, but I trust it's where I need to be. This is a short excerpt from one of my own journeys.

> *Visiting the Land of Tarot, I walked down a path and to the right was a woman in a white robe, her foot on a crescent moon. She was holding a drum. I asked if she was the*

High Priestess, and she said she was. I asked what she was doing here. She told me that I was having problems staying grounded with my meditation, so she was there to help me. She told me to continue down the path, and around the next bend I'd come to a walled town, and then I'd be in a field. I asked why she wore a crown of shimmering stars. She said it was because she was guided by divinity.

When I've journeyed to the Land of Tarot, I've taken the time upon returning to write what I saw, who I talked to, and what we spoke about. I'm almost always surprised at what I see and even more by what I learn—not only about the people but about myself.

When you return from your Land of Tarot, give yourself some time to describe this place in as much detail as possible. If you can sketch, all the better. The process is simple, but what can come out of it can be profound. Allow yourself the time and space to think about what you experienced.

You can return to the Land of Tarot time and again as you work through these pages, and anytime thereafter.

Once you've been to the Land of Tarot, the cards will begin to tell their stories in a way you've yet to hear.

One of these days I'll tell you about the Six of Pentacles who was handing out free pizzas.

THE TOOLS

More than Just Tarot

Tarot is my favorite tool for ancestral work, but it's not the only one. In this chapter I'm going to introduce you to the many tools that are used in communicating with magical ancestors. You may already know one or two, but give them all a browse as each can be valuable as you work with the magic ones in Part II.

Tarot

Almost everyone begins their tarot journey using a standard Rider-Waite-Smith (RWS) deck or a clone. It's a good starter deck and, in fact, may be *your perfect deck* for working with magical ancestors.

However, doing ancestral work really does require a deck that *feels* right. While I'm in love with modern, abstract decks like the inkblot-inspired *Hidden Waters*, those decks aren't easy for this work—at least for me. I work with *The Relative Tarot* by Carrie Paris (Red Wheel/Weiser 2021). I also use *Wheel of the Year Tarot, Witches' Wisdom,* and *DruidCraft*

Tarot. This isn't to say these are the decks *you* should use; they're just ones I'm comfortable with and have been using for a long time.

I'm going to harp about deck choice because it is so important. Let me share a couple of approaches for selecting a deck for this work.

First, choose a deck that has visual appeal. Before spending money sight unseen, search online for images or ask about them in an online tarot forum. When you find card images, do you feel drawn to the art style, the time period, and the colors?

How a deck looks and feels is superimportant to me as I don't respond intuitively to decks that are ultradark or those done in pastels. I love decks with bright and bold colors—which is weird, as *The Relative Tarot* is neither and yet it's my first choice for ancestral work.

Another thing to consider is the era depicted. If you connect with Renaissance Europe, you may not be all that comfortable with an indigenous-themed deck.

Do you feel the best deck for ancestral magic is something other than a standard *RWS*, like the Tarot of Marseilles? This deck's suits are the same as *RWS* but are written in French: Bâtons (Batons), Épées (Swords), Coupes (Cups), and Deniers (Coins). The Court cards in a TdM are titled Valet (Page), Chevalier (Knight), Dame (Queen), and Roi (King). The pips or minor suit cards are unillustrated. That means instead of seeing an illustrated scene like the beggars outside the church (Five of Pentacles), you'll simply have five coins.

I don't know about you, but I like illustrated pips because my interpretation riffs off the scene. Just seeing five coins doesn't mean anything to me, other than the basic *RWS* meaning.

Another consideration is the culture or ethnicity depicted in a deck. Does it feel familiar or comfortable to you? If you want a deck that reflects your own ethnicity, there are several decks that are specific to different countries. (See the chart a little later in this chapter.)

It's difficult to find decks that are 100% on point for a culture unless you're native to that country or culture. For example, there are "African Tarot" decks, but Africa is a continent, not a country. Still, if that's your genetic homeland, you may choose such a deck because you're unlikely to find a specifically Senegalese or Côte d'Ivoire tarot.

The Hoodoo Tarot, a deck for Rootworkers, is geared to the practice among early African Americans. The images are not of a colonial era but instead of how the practice has evolved over time and been handed down through generations. Many of the images are of real people, such as Aunt Caroline (who appears on Major Arcana 10), a cartomancer who was freed from slavery in 1865.

The *Dust II Onyx: A Melanated Tarot Deck* comes about as close to capturing African ancestral energies as I—as a white person—can understand. Each card is a work of art.

There is a whole host of Eurocentric decks, particularly those of the Celtic heritage found across the British Isles. Most witch-related decks are nature-based save for the *Modern Witch Tarot*, which depicts young witches in a modern city. (See the Queens in Chapter 2.)

Suggested tarot decks by continent (sorry, Antarctica):

NORTH AMERICA	SOUTH AMERICA	AFRICA	EUROPE
African American Tarot	Afro-Brazilian	Adinkra Ancestral Guidance Cards	Arthurian Tarot
Conjure Cards	Legitimo	African Goddess Rising	DruidCraft Tarot
Hoodoo Tarot	Mayan Oracle	African Tarot	Llewellyn Tarot
Mexican Tarot	Mayan Tarot	Ancient Wisdom Oracle Cards	Modern Witch
New Orleans Voodoo	Napo Tarot	Da Brigh African Tarot	Spanish Tarot
Santa Muerte (Mexico)	Tarot Namur	Dust II Onyx	Tarot de Marseilles
Tarot Yohualli Ehécatl		Tazama African Tarot	Wildwood Tarot
Vision Quest			

ASIA	AUSTRALIA	SPECIALIZED TOPICS
Aum Tarot	Aboriginal Dreamtime Oracle	Deviant Moon Tarot
Buddha Tarot	Aboriginal Spirit Oracle	Dragon Tarot
China Tarot	Animal Dreaming Oracle	Goddess Tarot
Fenestra Tarot	Australian Animal Tarot	Halloween Tarot
Golden Dragon Tarot	Far Sight Lenormand	Tarot of Baseball
I Ching Holitzka Deck	Far Sight Tarot	Tattoo Tarot
Southeast Asian Myths and Stories Tarot	Southern Cross Oracle	Vampire Tarot

Doing ancestral work using tarot guarantees surprises, some of which relate to the deck itself. It really does make a difference which one you choose. Let me tell you why.

I was working with a friend and asked that she pick a deck that she felt was the best for ancestral work. She chose the *Inner Child Cards*, which is a favorite of mine although not one she had used before. Not to get into her stuff, but a key to what she was working on was the Eight of Swords. An *RWS* Eight of Swords shows a blindfolded woman whose hands are bound surrounded by eight swords. However, the *Inner Child* deck depicts eight children walking through a dark and scary cave, holding swords with each tip lit like a torch. So, instead of being blindfolded and tied up, this deck shows the children bringing light into the darkness and finding their way out of the cave.

It's the same card, but with two vastly different ways to interpret the message.

I suggest playing with a few decks. You'll quickly learn if they work or not. You'll know by how they feel and how you feel using them. And remember what John B. said about how fussy the ancestors are about the deck—They are.

Since you'll be working through multiple exercises in Part II of this book—and not all of them tarot—I also want to introduce you to a few other tools you will be using.

Supplementary Cards

Supplementary cards are ones you'll need to make and use throughout your ancestral magic work. Although your ancestors will show up for you as Court cards, you won't always know their gender, the time in which they lived, or where they lived. You also won't know if they were family in another life.

The easiest way to determine these important unknowns is to make a batch of supplementary cards using index cards. First, draw a female symbol on one card and a male symbol on an other.

Next, using more index cards, write the number of a century on each card, e.g., 18 for the 18th century. Make as many of these century cards as you want. Once I reach a certain number of centuries back in time, I stop numbering and simply make an index card called Ancient One.

Using these supplementary cards, you can now find the gender of your Court card ancestor as well as the time period in which they lived. I then make one last card: the Past Life card. If I draw this card, it tells me the ancestor I'm working with was an ancestor or close to me in another life.

Another important tool is the pendulum.

Working with Pendulums

I want to talk about pendulums and the important role they play throughout the book. This is especially true in April in Part II, when you work with land magic.

In simplest terms, a pendulum is a weighted object attached to the end of a string. In our metaphysical world the pendulums you'll find in stores are made of a semiprecious stone attached to a slender metal chain.

You'll find pendulums made of many different stones, including lapis lazuli, tigereye, quartz crystal, jasper, and amethyst. The best one for doing ancestor work is *the one that wants to work with you.*

If you're in a metaphysical shop that sells pendulums, pick up several and try them out. Some swing instantly; some are motionless. My friend Fred had difficulty finding a pendulum that would move. Finally, he tried one made from pyrite, and it moved immediately. Maybe because pyrite is considered a stone with male energy. Compare pyrite to rose quartz and I think you'll immediately sense a difference in their energies.

If you don't want to buy a pendulum, you can easily make one. In fact, if I'm out and about, I'll use whatever's on hand. You'll need a piece of heavy twine or a metal chain. A metal chain works better just because of the weight. In a pinch, you can use a necklace. The pendulum itself can be a metal washer or any object that has some weight to it, such as a ring.

You can also go to any store that makes keys and request one that was miscut and they're going to throw away. The brass ones make great pendulums.

After you put together your pendulum, take it for a few test runs, as I'll outline next, in order to calibrate it.

So how do pendulums play into ancestral work?

First, they're great for asking yes/no questions. Here's how to calibrate your pendulum. When you first buy a pendulum, have a conversation asking it to show you which direction it swings for yes, no, and maybe. Although some books will tell you that yes is always a line moving away from your body and no is a line across your body, I've found that every pendulum has its own way of speaking.

If you're brand-new to pendulums, here's a quickie how-to: Hold the top of the chain between your thumb and index finger with the chain hanging free. Try not to hold your pendulum in a death grip. A light touch is all it takes. Let it swing as it will. Once it's stopped moving, you can begin to calibrate it to your own energy. First, ask it which direction it moves when giving you a "yes"; then repeat for "no" and "maybe."

Work with your new pendulum until you're superclear about which responses mean yes, no, and maybe. You can ask it questions you know the answers for to confirm you have the right responses. Once that's been determined, those are the directions that will always be in effect. Your pendulum will not swing one way for yes today and another way tomorrow. Your pendulum is now calibrated to you and your energy.

Other than using a pendulum to discern gender and a time period, I frequently use it in mapping. In ancestral work, the pendulum tells me where my ancestor lived. First, I will ask a quick yes/no question about each continent. Once I know the continent, I pull up a digital map on my tablet and let the pendulum lead me to the country. Once you get the hang of it, this is a quick process that can deliver a massive amount of useful information.

If you've been out of school for a long time and don't remember the continents, they are:

Europe

Australia

Asia

Africa

Antarctica

North America

South America

I don't think you're going to find an ancestor indigenous to Antarctica, unless you go back about 90 million years, but that was long before humans were on Earth.

Something to keep in mind if you use a pendulum for yes/no questions is to be sure to phrase the question in a way that results in an accurate answer. Avoid more general phrasings like "will *xyz* happen?" The better question would be: "Is there a way for me to make *xyz* happen this month?" If you don't ask a specific question, you may get a yes without realizing that yes won't happen for ten years . . .

Pendulums are also wonderful for picking cards. Let's say you've chosen a Court card to represent your ancestor for the month of August. Next, you've drawn three to five additional cards asking for the ancestral energy that best matches your own. Pick up your pendulum and let it hang over each of the cards. Now, your pendulum is going to behave differently from mine, but you'll feel subtle or not-so-subtle vibrations or movements from one card to the next.

If my pendulum wants to choose a card, its reaction is so strong it almost jumps out of my hand. When there's no energy connection over a card, it won't move at all.

Without getting into a whole book about pendulums, I do want to make one more suggestion. Get a piece of paper and lay it down in landscape orientation. Write on the paper whatever it is that you want the pendulum to respond to. For example, let's say you want to know which type of magic a specific ancestor can help you with. If the information you have gotten from your tarot cards isn't clear, let your pendulum lead you to the answer. List the different types of magic that have come up for you, drawing a fan shape, and then hold your pendulum over each one to see how it responds.

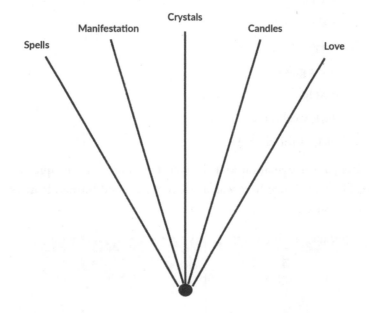

The same type of pendulum board can be drawn on a chalkboard easily purchased at a craft store. With a chalkboard you can create the layout you want, then erase it when you want to ask another set of questions. For instance, one set may have to do with the chakras while another with forms of magic or healing modalities.

If you don't want to create a new pendulum drawing in your grimoire each time, you can also DIY a more permanent pendulum board using a lightweight piece of wood from a craft store (mine cost $1). Then, wood burn indicators at intervals that you can define differently each time you need to. This way you can use the board repeatedly.

Pendulum boards can be used for many types of questions, including identifying:

- angelic entities
- female
- male
- fairy
- spirit guide
- past life
- days, weeks, months, years
- each of the chakras

Use your imagination to make your board relate to the questions you have. The one shown here was made using a wood burner. It marks percentage points.

Oracle Cards

I admit it. I have a love-hate thing with oracle cards. I think it's because I've used tarot for such a long time, or maybe because I love the art on oracles but want to interpret them my own way and find the titles to be distracting. Who knows? It's just one of those quirky things. While tarot exists within a specific system of seventy-eight cards, four suits, twenty-two Major Arcana, sixteen Court cards, forty Minor Arcana, an oracle deck has no such constraints, on either the number of cards or structure. Right now, an oracle I'm creating has forty-five cards and may go as high as sixty. It's up to the creator—and, of course, how much it costs to have the deck printed.

I've thought a lot about how useful oracle cards can be when doing ancestral tarot or working with ancestral magic. I found they often add a new—and valuable—layer of interpretation to readings.

First, you can use an oracle as a clarifier. We've all pulled tarot cards and then drawn a blank on what it means. Here's an example: you've asked an ancestor to help you with your manifestation skills and draw the Knight of Wands and the Ten of Swords.

I can see myself scratching my head about this pair. The Knight is telling me to get a move on, and yet the ten swords are keeping me pinned to the ground. I *think* I'm being told that my block isn't in my ability but with my thinking (the swords). It's hard to do magic if your brain tells you you're just imagining things. This is when to pull an oracle card to clarify.

From my own oracle-in-process, I pulled the Brick Wall. Clearly, that Knight is going nowhere until those negative thoughts are dealt with.

The second way you can use oracles with ancestral magic is in learning more about an ancestor. If you meet someone at a gathering in real life, you have a conversation to find out more about each other. An oracle deck can be like that. The oracle you choose will make just as much of a difference as a tarot deck. For me, it's hard to have a get-to-know-you conversation if my oracle only has pictures of herbs because I'm fairly ignorant about herbs. However, if I use a deck that shows sacred sites or people from the past, then I'm golden. Deck choice matters.

If you're working with an ancestor whose magic was related to the fae, then use a fairy oracle deck; if dragons, a dragon deck; if plant magic, an herbal deck. Once you know the magical being coming through, you'll know which type of deck to use. If you're unsure of the kind of magic the ancestor could manifest, use your pendulum.

Casting

Casting kits are comprised of small metal tokens in a variety of shapes—like scissors, hands, boats, birds, or money. You can toss them and interpret the message depending on where they land. Usually, a casting board is used, although you can cast on the floor, on paper, or in a box instead.

A casting board has defined areas so that you can interpret the cast by seeing which charms land on which defined areas. For example, if a heart lands on a part of a board referencing work, you'd interpret the cast differently than if it landed on the love part of the board. Just like you can put your own definitions on a pendulum board, you can make your own casting board with any number of sections important to you, ranging from everyday life to magical life. Parts of the board could be:

- self
- family
- money
- love
- moon phases
- candle magic
- chakras
- past lives

Carrie Paris, the creator of *The Relative Tarot*, often creates free downloadable casting sheets. You'll find her website in Appendix A. Once you see an example of a casting sheet, you'll have a better idea of how to create one of your own. You'll also find examples on Pinterest.

In addition to casting charms, I also use five small, polished stones—one for each of the inner planets (Mercury, Venus, Mars, Jupiter, Saturn). I begin with a question or intention, then cast the stones on the floor and note where they fall. Is Jupiter—the planet of expansion and luck—far away from me? Bummer. Is Mars (action/energy) sitting right next to Mercury (communication)? Then don't avoid having that tough conversation.

I also cast astrology dice. Their faces show planet, sign, and house. Have a question, then toss the dice. I think you might be surprised at how accurate these can be. You can also purchase inexpensive six-sided blank wooden dice at a craft store and create your own casting charms, dice, or symbols. Anything goes since what is important is your connection with the symbols used.

Sigils

A sigil is a symbol or combination of symbols that represents a desired outcome.

Look around you and you'll see symbols in use everywhere, like dollar signs, four-leaf clovers, hearts, or as logos. Using symbols is one way to create a sigil; another is working with an alphanumeric chart. Here's how to do both.

Method 1

This technique for generating sigils is based solely on symbolism. Remember the symbol for a house you drew in grade school? If it looked anything like mine, it was a square with a door and two windows. No matter how poor the art, everyone could tell it was a house.

I'll use the concept of healing as an example. If you think about the symbols you associate with healing, what are they? Possibly:

- a flower
- a heart
- a caduceus

- a snake
- the sun
- the moon

The symbols are going to mirror your feelings about healing. Once you have one or more symbols in mind, combine them, always working with an intent. My sigil became a combination of a stylized tree overlaid with a heart. (No joking about my lousy art skills!)

Spend a bit of time drawing the symbols that mean healing for you, then see what you can combine that feels like your intent. This is a sigil.

Method 2

Another method for crafting sigils is based on associating letters with numbers, then using them to generate a sigil. It sounds harder than it is.

These are the numerology equivalents to letters. Here's a quick list for reference:

1	2	3	4	5	6	7	8	9
a, j, s	b, k, t	c, l, u	d, m, v	e, n, w	f, o, x	g, p, y	h, q, z	i, r

Now, sketch a nine-panel grid that looks like this:

1	2	3
4	5	6
7	8	9

Next comes the fun part—choosing a single word or two that represent what magical healing means for you. After you have your word, you're going to sketch it in the grid using the numbers associated with the letters after eliminating any repeating numbers. For example, if my word has two fives, I only use one of them. Let me show you how to do it using an example:

The words I came up with are *Star Energy*. Using the alphabet to numbers chart, my letters for *Star Energy* are 1-2-1-9-5-5-5-9-7-7. Since I don't want any repeating numbers, I'm left with 1-2-9-5-7. Now I'm ready to create my sigil. I begin in the 1 square, and then draw a continuous line that touches all the appropriate squares in order, like so:

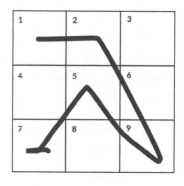

Note that I leave a little tail on the end in the 7 square. Now I can transfer this sigil to anything I want, including paper, my skin, a wooden disk, soap, my food, or even taped to my fridge door if my healing includes eating better.

Which method appeals to you?

Sidewalk Oracles

A sidewalk oracle is a message received when you're out in the neighborhood—any neighborhood. A sidewalk oracle, for me, is generally used as a clarifier, or an additional message layered on top of one I've already received.

Sidewalk oracles are like signs or omens. They have their origin in Roman augury, which was a form of bird divination. The Roman augurs based their predictions on bird behavior, like how a bird flew or whether it ate food left out for it. But since Julius Caesar isn't looking over our shoulders, I'll just say that doing a sidewalk oracle is an effective and valuable way to look for signs. Plus, no birds are harmed.

I think one of the most valuable aspects of doing sidewalk oracles is in answering the questions they themselves generate. For instance, I saw a gorgeous red hibiscus and it occurred to me that red is a color that tells us to *go!* But if it's in a traffic signal, it means *stop!* When I saw that hibiscus, why did those definitions of *stop* and *go* come to mind? What was the underlying message or omen? Think about it.

Although I mostly work with sidewalk oracles, I also use the method of standing barefoot in my doorway at dawn—or as close to it as possible—listening and looking for signs. British author Caitlin Matthews is quite expert at this. (For more on her see Appendix A.) If you go back to the Introduction, you'll see this was what I was doing on the morning of February 1, as I wrote the first words of this book. Caitlin suggests writing something that will remind you of what you experienced.

On that morning, I wrote:

> *Gentle wind blowing from the west, home of Bear, my spirit animal.*
>
> *Crows chattering in the west.*
>
> *Daylilies swaying*
>
> *Surface of the water in a small fountain rippling like waves on the sea*
>
> *Blue skies, light puffy clouds*
>
> *Sparrows in the east*
>
> *Smell of after-rain*
>
> *Sound of lingering raindrops dripping*
>
> *A door closed, a door opened, a door closed.*

You may or may not make omens part of your own practice, but if nothing more, try to track them in your grimoire. Today, the sound of a helicopter may mean nothing to you, but a month from now the sound may trigger a memory that relates to your ancestral work. Don't be afraid to use sidewalk oracles or omens to predict. It's all good practice.

Runes and Rune Decks (Optional)

I'm going to tell you right up front that I am not a rune expert or even a rune beginner. But I do know people who are excellent rune historians and readers, like John Hijatt. According to John, *"Runes are probably better used as clarifiers because they don't speak much to characteristics like tarot does.*

Possibly with a lot of work and time, one could use the runes to do ancestral work, but it would take a person who is very experienced with the runes, mythology, practice, and stories."

With my limited knowledge of runecraft, I can say that using them for clarification works for me, even though I have to look up the meanings. Although I don't know them that well (I'm learning), they can add another layer of interpretation.

While you'll often seen runes either carved into wood disks or engraved into some other material like clay, glass, plastic, or metal, there are rune decks. Some of them depict only the image of the rune itself, while others show a scene that relates to the rune. For example, the *Runes for Modern Life* card for Laguz pictures a surfer sitting on his board with sea turtles close by. He looks like he's enjoying sitting in the flow of the ocean. The rune for this card translates as the Lake or the Ocean.

I think runes can tell us about a facet of an ancestral life or their magical practice, but—at least for me—they don't help me understand personality.

Lenormand (Optional)

Like oracles, Lenormand decks can be used to tell us something about an ancestor's life. If you've never used Lenormand, it's a European-based deck of thirty-six cards. They don't have the layers of meaning that you'll find in tarot, though. The system is more suited to giving you straightforward answers to your questions. In a way it's a bit like the Queen of Swords in that she is direct and to the point. (See Appendix B for Lenormand keywords.)

Here's one way to use Lenormand—or oracles, for that matter—that I've found to be not only helpful but also fascinating as it gives me a glimpse into a key component of my magical ancestor's life. I draw three cards while asking for more information on an ancestor's magical abilities. For instance, I drew three cards from the Bear Lenormand (my own deck, a work in progress) and got Snake, Heart, and Key.

If you don't know Lenormand:

Snake = stealth, betrayal, treachery

Heart = love, generosity, compassion

Key = solution, opportunity, unlocked secrets

If you drew these three cards, how would you interpret them relative to the question about magical abilities? Try to read the line of three as a little story.

I might say that this ancestor's magic (key) was grounded in spells that warded off betrayal in love. What do you think?

Another use for a Lenormand deck is in conjunction with your pendulum. Using these same three cards, I asked which of the three cards was the one I should take to the Land of Tarot for more information.

Both the Snake and the Heart caused the pendulum to swing in a small clockwise direction. The Key, however, jerked the pendulum as though it were being pulled by an unseen hand.

How then to work with the Key? Personally, I'd look through the tarot deck to see where I can find a key. I know the Hierophant has two of them at his feet. So on my next visit to the Land of Tarot, I'd try to track down the Hierophant.

Energy Work

In the grand scheme of things, energy work may be the most important aspect of this work.

Magical tools are not, in themselves, magical. For instance, a tarot card is not magical. It is a piece of paper with a picture on it. What is magical, though, is the energy coming off the card.

Let me give you an easy way to wrap your head around energy. Think of watching TV and seeing an ad for pizza or the latest gizmo or a new line of KitchenAid appliances. None of those objects are magical, but they work magic on you because you want to pick up the phone and order the pizza or start checking stores for the gizmo or a new kitchen toy. The images trigger a response. Magic is a combination of intent and energy made manifest. Well, those advertisers had an intent (to sell you something), they put energy into their intent (they created an ad), and magically now they have manifested you as a customer. Yes, sometimes it's just that easy.

When you work through the chapters of Part II, using tarot, oracles, your pendulum, runes, or Lenormand, you're adding the energy of the objects to your own energy and intent. The magic may not happen immediately, but now it's out rolling around the Enchantosphere building to manifestation.

Keep in mind that your interest leads to intent, which leads to magic. If your interest in working with land magic is *meh*, it's not going to get much, if any, energy. So that means no magic. But if manifestation is your thing, your interest and intent will draw in energy to create a powerhouse of magic.

Of course, all this is easier to do than talk about, so let's get moving.

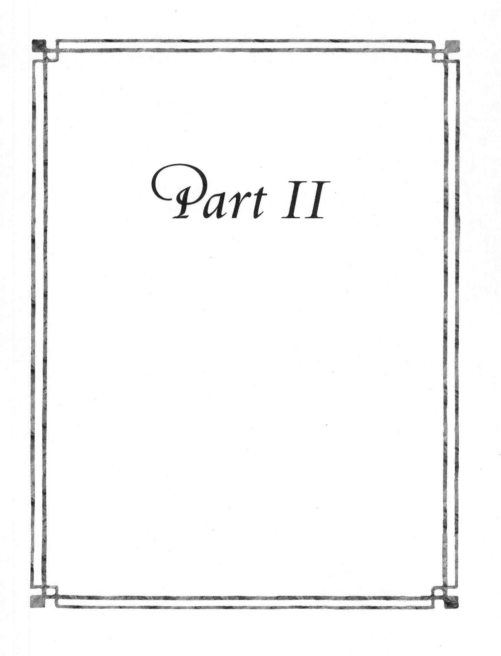

Part II

A YEAR OF ANCESTORS

Create Your Ancestral Grimoire

Ancestors come in all shapes, sizes, and abilities. Some were in your blood-line while incarnate, others were friends or family in multiple other life-times. Taken together, the number of ancestors personal to you counts in the millions and beyond. Of those, who knows how many practiced a form of magic?

There's a funny thing about ancestors. You know that your body car-ries bits and pieces of their DNA, but did you know that tucked in that DNA are skills as well as physical characteristics? If you've ever heard your mom say, "You're just like Grandma," then you have an inkling about the DNA thing. If Mom was referencing Granny's ability to grow the biggest tomatoes in the neighborhood, it's likely your skills in gardening or kitchen witchery came directly from that family line.

Because most of us never knew ancestors beyond our grandparents, we have only a tiny swatch of knowledge from which to draw. You may know that your dad and granddad are cornhole champs, but who knows if your Scottish grandfather ten generations back was a champion caber tosser.

When it comes to inherited magic, finding evidence through research is virtually impossible. Unless, of course, you know that an ancestor fell to one of the witch trials rumbling across Europe and in America.

But if you're here now, I know with certainty that at least one magical skill has been carried through generations in your DNA. You may already know that skill and want to improve on it, discover it, or branch out into other forms of magic that enhance your practice.

How Do You Know?

We humans have an incredible capacity for tapping into genetic memory. I know that sitting around a campfire on the chilliest of autumn nights is comfortingly familiar because we have a genetic—or ancestral—memory of doing the same thing all the way back to the days when we first discovered fire.

Encoded into your DNA are survival skills you rarely need, but your body remembers when you did. If scared, without a moment of conscious thought you go into fight-or-flight mode. That cave bear is no longer chasing you, but your body remembers the fear.

Did you know that encoded into that same DNA are a multitude of skills perfected over generations? Some are physical like running fast or singing in perfect pitch. But others are less noticeable—and less talked about. One skill is being able to pick up a crystal and innately understand its specific energy. Another is a certainty that praying to a household saint always brings in unexpected money.

Magic at its core is the investment of intent and energy into creation. You already know how to do it—but it's possible you just forgot the way. Fortunately, you're not starting from scratch because somewhere, in one of those DNA strands, is the magic that is yours to claim.

Gather Your Tools

Your initial meeting with each ancestor may vary by month. But typically, you'll begin by drawing a Court card. If you're stumped on interpreting the Court as an ancestor, go back to Chapter 2. Read the upright and reversed meanings, then relate the card to someone you know in real life. The more characteristics you can relate to each card, the easier they will be to read. If you know that the Page of Cups is your sister, then you have a good idea of how that ancestor is showing themselves to you.

Throughout the following chapters you'll also be using the whole tarot deck, an oracle deck, and a pendulum, as well as (optionally) Lenormand and runes. There are also a few DIY projects and a time or two of using crystals. I encourage you to let yourself off the logic hook and allow your intuition to play a major role in doing this work.

Not all ancestors will be a good fit for you. I'm sure some of them work in areas for which you have little or no interest. In those cases, you can skip to another chapter. But I hope you go ahead and do the tarot spreads and other exercises anyway. The more you work with the ancestors, the easier and more natural it becomes.

There's one other thing. Some readers prefer relating a specific Court card with an ancestor they knew. For example, one friend always knows that it's her grandmother coming through if she draws the Queen of Cups. If you want to assign certain Court cards to specific ancestors, that works too.

The Four Types of Magic

If you're into astrology, you already know about planetary rulerships. For example, Mercury rules Virgo and Mars is the ruler of Aries. The next twelve chapters follow a similar line, but instead of each being ruled by a planet, they're ruled by one of your ancestors.

Each ancestor can work a certain type of magic. During their incarnation they may have had extraordinary skills. Or they may have tried and failed or had only minimal success. Until you explore the ancestor's life, you won't know which. Why would an ancestor who failed be the one to come forward to you? Because they want to help you avoid the same mistakes they did.

You'll be visiting twelve realms in four areas of magic. Each of those realms has its own ancestors, but if you want to work with the same ancestor all year—or even ask for a thirteenth ancestor who will guide you through the book—those are also paths you can take. Much of ancestral work is based on intuition—so trust yours.

Although the book is designed for you to work with each month as it occurs in real time, there's also nothing stopping you from going directly to the area of magic that interests you the most. I'm too much of an Aries moon to stop anyone from skipping around. The four areas, each of which will have three months here, are:

FAMILY MAGIC	PERSONAL MAGIC	ELEMENTAL MAGIC	CELESTIAL MAGIC
January Inherited Magic	February Manifestation Magic	April Land Magic	May Moon Magic
November Ancestral Magic	March Healing Magic	July Weather Magic	June Solstice Magic
December Magical You	August Past Life Magic	October Omen Magic	September Sky Magic

It's my hope that as you work through each chapter, you'll transfer all your practices, spreads, and personal and family magic to your own Book of Shadows. This will guarantee that you amass a magical collection that is personal to you. No one on this planet—or off it—will have the same book.

Once you've finished all twelve months, I don't think you'll ever see yourself in the same way again.

Daily Draws

At the end of each chapter, you'll find suggestions for daily draws or journal ideas. They're all built around the ancestor who came forward for you as well as the magic explored during the month.

If you do the daily draws, try to interpret your cards as they relate to the month's energies. For example, if you're working with Manifestation

Magic (Personal Magic/February) and your daily draw is Temperance (Major Arcana 14), how does that relate to the ancestor or what you're trying to manifest? If your manifestation goal is a better work environment, how about adding flowers or a tabletop fountain to your desk. Why? Because Temperance is typically shown standing in front of an iris, with one foot in the water.

Use the symbols on your daily draws to begin embedding their energy into your work. If you journal using this technique, you'll quickly see your skills improving. Is it magic born from thin air? Nope. Your willingness to merge clear intent with energy is what powers your magic.

Which One Holds Your Ancestors

One thing I do every morning is ask the ancestors for a message. This is my process: For me, the Six of Cups is always the card that represents the ancestors—not just for today but always. In the morning, I shuffle the entire deck and then draw down from the top until I get to the Six of Cups. Then the next card in the deck is the daily message. If my Six of Cups is the last card in the deck, the message is the card that was on top of the deck.

This is a powerful draw because it's a way that the ancestors can directly communicate their messages. If you decide to do this practice, assign your own marker card like my Six of Cups that *you* feel most represents *your* ancestors. Then shuffle and begin drawing down in the deck till you reach your ancestor card. The next card is your message.

Let's move on to January.

JANUARY

Family Magic: Inherited Magic

January Tools

- ✧ tarot
- ✧ pendulum
- ✧ sidewalk oracles

Your Intergenerational Magic

You are the latest in a family line of inherited magic. What better way to begin the new year than to meet an ancestor who shares your bloodline as well as your inheritance?

My guess is, you may already have a sense of your family's magical skills, even though it hasn't been obvious for generations. I believe, deep down, we all know from an early age what draws us in and what repels us. Let me give you an example.

I once saw an oracle card that depicted a Hopi emerging from an underground kiva, his body silhouetted against the Pleaides and a shooting star. That image stayed with me for years. But the closest I came to seeing that sky myself was on a winter stargazing trip in Northern Arizona.

That wasn't the first time the stars called me, though; my folks gave me a little telescope when I was just ten, and my love of the sky has never waned. It seemed to me then and even now that my ancestral magic comes from the stars. But where did it begin?

You know, the sky I saw on that Arizona night wasn't much different from the one your own ancestors would have seen. Orion still dominates the winter night sky. Venus is there too—her phases as visible as the moon's if you have a pair of binoculars. And in your ancestor's time, as now, the great Andromeda Galaxy skirts the edge of the Milky Way.

January marks the middle of winter. In the Northern Hemisphere night comes early, and darkness reigns even in early morning. It's as if Mother Nature herself supports this as a time for looking at what we've kept hidden, even from ourselves. To me, it seems that now is as good a time as any to peer into the shadows and see who's there. If I heard my own ancestors correctly, I'm fairly certain I know who's knocking at *your* door. If you're as curious as I am, read on.

The One Who Waits

My guess is this ancestor has been waiting for you for a very long time. There are at least two ways for you to find out who this is and to make a connection.

> **Method 1:** Go into the Land of Tarot (Chapter 4) and trust that the person you meet is the person you're meant to meet. It could be a Court card, a Minor Arcana person, or an archetypal Major Arcana. If you choose this method, trust me, the ancestor will come forward to meet you.

> **Method 2:** Separate your tarot deck into Court cards, Major Arcana, and Minor Arcana. Shuffle each pile and from the Court cards randomly draw one card, *being clear about your intent*. In case you've forgotten, your intent is to meet the ancestor whose magic has been passed down through your own bloodline.

Before reading further, stop and find this ancestor, then write down what you learn in your grimoire. Use the supplementary cards you made in Chapter 5 to define gender and era. Then, use your pendulum to discover where they lived. Answer the following questions in your January pages:

- ⁘ Who appeared?

- ⁘ Did you draw a card or do a visualization?

- ⁘ If you drew a card, was it upright or reversed?

- ⁘ Is this an ancestor you knew in real life? (That's if you drew a 21- or 20th-century supplementary card.)

- ⁘ How would you interpret this card as a magical person in your lineage?

I encourage you to record all this now because it's so easy to forget your first impressions, but they are central to your intuitive response.

Remember: if you draw a reversed Court, you're seeing the shadow side of this ancestor. If you do get a reversal, ask *why* your ancestor is showing you their shadow side. A reversal doesn't mean the ancestor is *only* a shadow-side person. Everyone has both upright and reversed qualities, but for some reason they want you to see the shadow. Why? Is it possible that this is an ancestor who has your magical lineage but failed to use it for good? Or, that they felt they had to hide their magic? I don't know the answer. It's something you'll have to ask.

So now you know the personality, gender, time period when this ancestor lived, and their approximate locale. Google that time and place to see what was up during this ancestor's life and get a fuller picture of their life.

Next, draw a Major Arcana card, asking for the archetypal energy of the ancestor. Although the Majors display twenty-two archetypes, there really are others that can fit into one or more of the cards. For example, a

Wanderer archetype can be the Fool but also the Moon, and an Altruist could show up as the Hanged Man (sacrifice) or the High Priestess (inner knowledge). The world's cultures and religions are filled with archetypes that we tap into all the time.

What is the archetypal energy of your January ancestor? Intuitively, how does this feel? If your magical ancestor stayed in the metaphysical closet, it's possible that the archetype may seem way off base, because it wasn't something your family ever discussed. How, then, would you even have an inkling about the magic? If this is the case in your family, it's natural that it may feel off base.

After using your tools, you now know even more about this ancestor, but do you know what magic they share with you? If you can't tell by the cards that you've already pulled, draw three to five Minor Arcana, and let your intuition guide you. Also, look at the suits you're drawing as the elements contain important clues. For example:

∴ Wands—Fire magic, like smoke divination or candle magic

∴ Cups—healing or scrying

∴ Swords—communication magic, maybe even bird whisperers

∴ Pentacles—land or money magic

Return to the Major Arcana card you drew as well and see if there are clues hidden in the card. For instance, the Moon (Major Arcana 18) is a watery card associated with Pisces, the Devil with earthy Capricorn, and the Magician with airy Mercury. If you don't know the astrological correspondences to the Majors, see Appendix B.

Still a Mystery?

If you still don't understand your inherited magical skill, try this:

Get your pendulum and a piece of paper or a chalkboard, and create a pendulum layout. Write the types of magic you think might be yours. Your board will look something like this, but the words will be your own.

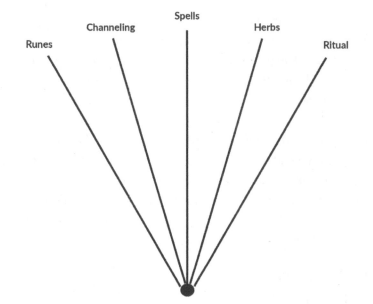

Next, use your pendulum and see if you get an energetic hit on any of the words. If your pendulum doesn't move at all, try different words. Or if it doesn't want to move along any of the lines, just hold it over each of the words and see what happens. It's possible that you may get a strong energetic pull on more than one type of magic.

Don't rush the process.

I'll Share This

I set my intent and asked for an ancestor whose magic I have inherited. I drew the Knight of Swords. That's cool as he's my favorite Knight.

I used my supplementary cards and pendulum to discover who he was and when he lived. The cards showed that he was a male who lived far before written history. I used the pendulum to put a pin in where he lived, and for the very first time my pendulum wouldn't budge.

I was beyond puzzled, so I drew a Major Arcana, hoping it would help me understand this ancestor's magic. Honestly, you won't believe me, but I promise it's true: The Major Arcana I drew was the Star. This gave me the shivers as it confirmed my belief in my own star magic.

I asked the Knight to tell me about his magic and drew the Ace of Wands. I could have drawn more cards if I needed to, but I knew this was the answer I was seeking. My magic, passed down through generations, is star magic—the magic of working with celestial energy to envision ideas (Knight of Swords), activate them (Ace of Wands), and then manifest (the Star). That my pendulum would not specify any place on Earth left me wondering if a sky being had popped in. More to discover . . .

Here's why I'm sharing this: I want you to know that it's okay to draw one card or many. Don't hesitate to dialogue with whoever shows up. Keep up the conversation until you understand the magic.

Practicing Your Skill

Once you accept your own magical lineage, you'll begin to see omens or signs everywhere that, weirdly, relate to your magic.

Sidewalk oracles (or omens) are one of the easiest ways to begin practicing and improving your skill, regardless of what it is. Instead of seeing a snowdrift, a trash truck, or a fence, you'll begin sensing each one of those objects as a message. The tarot is limited to seventy-eight messages; the world of sidewalk oracles has an infinite number.

Are you open to a little augury? Take a turn outside and see what you find. The intent here is to gain more information about your inherited magic.

Now, I don't want you looking at bird entrails, but I do want you to pay attention to the birds themselves. Keep an eye out for things like:

- direction of flight
- bird species
- flying solo or in a group
- color
- song or no song

Remember the augury used by the Romans? Apply your newly found skills to work with bird energy. For example, if a bird is flying west, what does that mean to you? For me, west is about going inside my bear cave. But the direction must be meaningful to *you*.

Consider the message about your magic that the birds could be telling you. Is your inherited magic dependent on others (flying in a group), or are you at your most powerful when flying solo? Look, too, at the color of the birds and the color you typically wear. Black only? Bright hues? White? What might that mean? If the birds are singing, is it sweet and melodious or harsh and cackling like the crow? What other messages do the birds carry? And what can you divine from them about your family's magical inheritance?

You'll have an entire month to work with this ancestor, the birds, your cards, and your pendulum. If you have a burning desire to become proficient at your inherited magic, then write about it, practice it, and take it out for a test drive. If you're not sure how, get out your pendulum and cards. And don't forget your intuition.

For example, if your inherited magic is working with herbs, but you don't know what to do next ... do an online search for medicinal or magical herbs, and try blending teas (be sure you know which herbs you're using; no poisonous ones, please!). Still not sure how to practice? Draw an oracle card. If you get a card like the Intuitive Moon, you may want to learn which moon phase is the most effective for your work (see May), or you may want to find plants that are associated with the moon. Honestly, you can work with your inherited magical skills for a lifetime, so there is no need to hurry. It takes time to build a skill.

I work with the star Arcturus. Even on cloudy nights I know where Arcturus is shining. My practice is as simple as visualizing a star–Nancy energy exchange and then directing that energy to whatever I'm working on.

Don't make it difficult.

If getting outdoors for a sidewalk oracle excursion is impractical in cases of ice, snow, blizzards, or other natural disincentives, invite the ancestor to sit and chat with you. Draw cards as needed to understand and practice your shared magic. Questions you may want to pose could be:

- ✧ Why have I inherited this magic?
- ✧ How can I work with you in improving my skills?
- ✧ How can this magic impact my everyday life?
- ✧ In what way can I incorporate this magic into my established practice?
- ✧ How do I use this magic?

I could tell you to use your intuition to better understand how to use your magic, but I know sometimes it's hard to believe what you're hearing. If this is you, draw a Major Arcana card, and then use your pendulum to understand the message.

For example, pretend you drew Judgement (Major Arcana 20). What are the symbols on an *RWS* version of that card?

- a trumpet
- a flag with a cross
- coffins
- mountains
- clouds
- trees
- women
- men
- children
- an angel
- blond hair
- red wings
- red in hair

Write down what you see and hold your pendulum over each word, or hold it over each section of the card. Do you pick up any clues from how the pendulum moves? When I did this exercise, my pendulum was most active over the flag. My intuition tells me to incorporate sigils (Chapter 5) into my star magic.

Do you see how all your skills working with cards, intuition, magic, and pendulum can play together?

Laser Beam, Not Shotgun

Before scooting off to another month, consider your obligations, expectations, and opinions. Losing focus is simple; keeping it going can be a challenge. So this month I'm going to ask you to create a card that symbolizes the energy of your familial magic.

You can base the card on a tarot or oracle card, or just follow your intuition.

Here's what you'll need:

A tarot or oracle card (optional)

An index card

Pictures of your choosing or drawing materials

Scissors

Glue

If you already have an intuitive hit on what should go on the card, go for it. If not, shuffle an entire tarot or oracle deck, asking what you need to know about sustaining and growing your inherited ancestral magic. If you pulled a card, don't try to copy the images, but do try to capture the energy and blend it with your own. Once created, you may want to tuck the card inside your grimoire or somewhere out of sight. It's personal and it's potent. It's possible this ancestor is one you'll work with for a lifetime or only a few weeks. And even if tomorrow's calendar turns over to February, no worries. They will still be here waiting for you.

Daily Draws

Draw a card daily or as often as you can asking for messages that can help you practice your inherited magic. Here are a couple of card readings to get you started with your own interpretations:

Three of Wands—how can you use three sticks in your magical practice?

Two of Pentacles—can you incorporate two coins into your magic?

Strength—no lions, please! But is there a cat who's willing to work with you on an energetic level?

Queen of Pentacles—Can you incorporate plants into your family magic?

Since I work with star energy, how would I incorporate plants? The first thing that came to mind was grinding some star anise and adding it to my tea or soup. Get the idea?

FEBRUARY

Personal Magic: Manifestation Magic

February Tools

- ⟡ tarot
- ⟡ postcard
- ⟡ manifestation log
- ⟡ manifestation jar
- ⟡ charm casting

Making Ideas Manifest

This month, you're going to delve into the magic of an ancestor who excelled at making real that which existed only in the mind. You're going to meet the Master Manifester.

Sometimes I think we all want to be like the Ancient Ones who envisioned the grand circle at Stonehenge, then made it manifest, even if it meant hauling bluestones from a Welsh quarry 140 miles distant. Your personal Stonehenge may not be as grand an undertaking, but it's no less a focal point for your internal solstices: a thriving business, healing family trauma, vibrant health, or raising compassionate children.

Once upon a long time ago, I sat on the banks of the Sandy River in Oregon and talked to a friend about my dreams. The biggest one was becoming a writer. I held on to that dream for years, through some jobs that fed the soul and others that sucked it dry. But that dream eventually became a reality. Now here's the truth of it: there's nothing special about my dream coming true. I wasn't better or smarter or more educated than anyone else who wanted the same thing. So how did it happen?

I could say that I'm stubborn, but the truth is, being a writer was always a true calling. I have an insatiable hunger for learning new things and then sharing them with others. It's like *Star Trek*'s Captain Kirk, whose first, best destiny was being a starship captain. Mine was working with words.

Your first, best destiny may be as a tarot reader, a kitchen witch, a spell-caster, or the best parent ever. You may excel at past life readings, have the Midas touch, or be a love guru. Regardless of the goal, my guess is you want to help others and excel at what you do. You also want your life and work to stand the test of time—just like those stones on the Salisbury Plain.

Unfortunately, you're going to run into people who will tell you that what you want can't be done. But if the desire is in alignment with your core and you do the work, it moves from the possible to the probable.

Let me share this: A friend of mine created a vision board onto which she glued all the things she wanted, including a Spanish-style house, a thriving business, and a solid relationship. She even pulled the Lovers card from one of her tarot decks and attached it to the board. About a year later I was sitting in her office, looking at the board hanging over her desk, and realized that everything she wanted had come true. She had gotten married, moved to a beautiful red tile–roofed Spanish-style house, and had clients coming to her consulting business. I don't think creating a vision board magically made things happen, but I do think things happened because her vision was sharp, she did the needed steps, and that vision was in alignment with who she was. Is that magic? I say yes, because her ideas became manifest.

Since many manifestations relate to money, let's talk about it. As spiritual as I am, I am still a pragmatist and curious about the whole manifesting thing. Years ago, I kept a little diary in which I wrote the dates and amounts of money or things that I gave away. Sometimes it was only a dollar tucked into a library book or a penny dropped on a curb. The amount didn't matter; for me it was testing the concept. (Did I mention I was born in the Show Me state?)

According to the diary—which I still have—almost every time I dropped a coin, something came back to me almost immediately, usually in no more than a day or two. Often it was more money, but sometimes it was a writing job or a neighbor offering to mow the lawn. It really was as simple as that. I had an intention, and I followed my intuition of what to do (energy) and trusted the outcome. And no, I'm not a devotee of *The Secret*. But I do believe in intention, putting in the work, and trusting that the ancestors will help me, provided it's for my highest good.

I think I've blabbed enough. So let's move into February's exploration. For this month, shuffle your entire deck and set an intention to meet an ancestor who can help you become a magical manifester. This is an ancestor who could envision a goal or a dream and then take the steps needed to bring it into being.

After shuffling, draw down from the top of the deck until you reach a Court card. This is the ancestor you'll be working with. Use your supplementary cards and pendulum to identify gender, time period, and approximate location. If you're foggy about the Court card's personality, go back to the descriptions in Chapter 2. Be sure to read both the upright and reversed positions.

After you've found your ancestor, draw a second card. This time you are looking for the Major Arcana. Reshuffle the entire deck and repeat the process of drawing down from the top until you reach a Major Arcana. This will represent your ancestor's manifestation ability.

Lastly, repeat the same process and find your first Minor Arcana card, asking for specifics of how this ancestor was able to manifest. Draw as many cards as you need to get clarity here.

If you're unfamiliar with how to translate a Major Arcana as a manifestation ability, look at the Major Arcana Correspondences in Appendix B. There you'll find the element each card (ancestral energy) is most comfortable and powerful using. For example, the Hierophant is most comfortable working with Earth energy, while the Death card is all about Water.

I'll Share This

I drew the King of Cups, for a male who lived in 14th-century Britain. When I drew a Major Arcana to learn more about his ability, I came to the Tower, which is associated with the element of Fire. You may remember that, astrologically, the King of Cups is associated with Scorpio—the most intense of signs. What kind of fire magic do you think a Scorpio would use? As this ancestor lived at the time of the Black Death, I have a feeling he used fire as a healing agent. Why healing? Cups are natural healers—at least for me.

I drew several Minor Arcana cards to show me how he worked his magic. Just to share one, I drew the Two of Swords. I didn't even try and interpret the card. Instead, I sat with my eyes closed and arms crossed, envisioning this ancestor at work. In my mind, I saw him sitting (as the figure on the card does), focusing an image of a healing fire helping the sick.

What I intuited from all this is my manifestation needs to include something relating to fire, like the color red or orange, a match, a holly berry, or a piece of flint.

What of your cards? Think about what you want to manifest. Then draw cards or use your pendulum to see exactly how this ancestor can help you. I encourage you *not to settle* for an ambiguous answer. Get something specific that you can do *today*. Then, try the method out all month—I'm a fan of finding the proof in the pudding. Once you see firsthand how an ancestor can help, it will make it far easier to trust the process in the future.

The Manifesting Spread

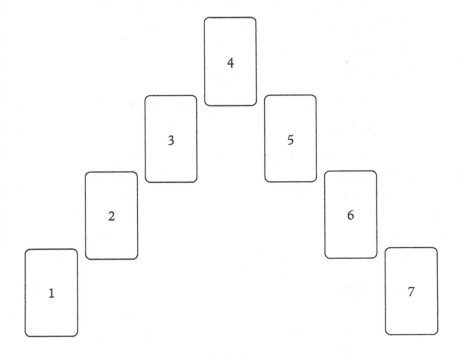

I think one of the coolest things about using a divination system in working with your ancestor is the ability to ask an unlimited number of questions. If something isn't clear, draw more tarot cards or use a different system like oracles, runes, or Lenormand.

For now, *start with something you want to manifest,* then use your tarot deck to do this spread. If any cards are unclear, go ahead and draw from a different divination system for clarification.

To begin, shuffle the entire deck, then draw from the top down. There's no need to separate your deck into Major-Minor-Court piles. Then read the cards based on these questions:

1. What does my ancestor feel about my goal?

2. What belief do I have about manifesting that might need healing?

3. What part of my manifestation plan needs more energy?

4. What needs my trust?

5. What is my unique manifestation magic?

6. How can I work closely with this ancestor to manifest?

7. What needs to stay frozen until later in the year?

For my own reading, the hardest message was position 4—what needs my trust. Interestingly, exactly what I'm trying to manifest fell in that position. The message was clear: I need to trust that what I want to manifest is right for me.

What position was most difficult for you? You're writing this in your grimoire, right?

Take an Alternate Approach

Do you want more information beyond the spread you just did? Choose an oracle that fits your goal. Since one of my goals is about writing, I used *The Literary Witches Oracle*. If you work with nature spirits, pick a nature deck. If you have only one deck, that's okay—trust that you'll receive the message you're meant to receive. For this draw, you're going to pull three cards:

1. What is at the heart of what I want to manifest?

2. Where do I lack clarity?

3. How can my ancestor help manifest?

I think position 1 is especially important because it's possible, at your core, what you *think* you want isn't *really* what you want. Play close attention to that one. What do I mean by that? You may *say* you want a new job, but what you're *really* asking for is respect and fair compensation. Position 1 holds the truth behind your desire.

Sometimes You Just Need to Ask

Do you remember writing to Santa when you were a kid? Sometimes that bike arrived on Christmas morning, or sometimes you got socks (thanks, Granny!). But as a kid, you didn't think twice about asking for what you wanted, did you?

As adults, we've learned to keep quiet about our wishes. Maybe you're embarrassed to verbalize your goals, or you think they're never going to happen so why bother?

But I'm an optimist. And I would like you to write a postcard to your magical manifesting ancestor, asking for what you want—a real postcard with real postage that you will really drop in the mailbox. (Keep track of when you send the card in your grimoire.)

I have a postcard I've been saving for an important occasion that shows the Milky Way over the Grand Canyon. I wrote my note to the King of Cups and addressed it to Britain, 14th century. Because I have such faith in the ancestors, I had quite a big ask—check back with me next year to see if it happened.

You understand this, right? It doesn't matter that the postcard can't be delivered. What matters is *the ask*.

Keep a Manifestation Log

Just like I did all those years ago, I'd like you to keep a manifestation log in your grimoire. I suggest two sections: Outgoing and Incoming.

In the Outgoing section write the date and what went out. Was it a book you left at the coffeehouse or a fiver tucked into a tip jar? One of my friends blesses a handful of pennies, then randomly drops them around town.

In the Incoming section, note all the goodness coming back to you, along with the date. What you receive can take many forms so it's impossible to list them all, but here's just a tiny sample of what might come:

∴ money—especially the unexpected kind

∴ a job

∴ a discount haircut

∴ a stranger paying the $5 you're short at the grocery store

∴ an offer of a new pair of jeans because your friend bought a size too small

∴ an invitation to a (paid) dinner on a night you're just too beat to even think about cooking

∴ a gift of a new deck of tarot cards

∴ winning a $5 lottery ticket

∴ a huge closeout deal at the appliance store on the day your fridge dies

The amount or the thing doesn't matter. What matters is how quickly you see the correlation between outgoing and incoming. It's a bonus if you use whatever technique the ancestor suggested—like my crossed arms and closed eyes.

A Manifesting Jar

I have a thing about not throwing away empty spice bottles. That's because they're a perfect size for a manifesting jar. Does that mean my goals are so tiny they only need a small jar? Nope. It just means I have a clear intent about the goal and the energy of what goes into the jar.

If you want a jar for more money, yours may be filled with coins, cinnamon, and basil. As tarot's Pentacles (Coins) are the suit of earthly things like money, go back through that suit and see if anything pops for you. A few of the symbols on Pentacles include fruit, flowers, feathers, wood, dirt, and glass.

If you want better health, add something from all the elements such as a tiny crystal (Earth), a piece of sage (Air), a bit of something orange or red (Fire), and purified water (Water). There's no limitation to what you add to the jar. The contents will be the things that carry the energy you wish to manifest.

The next time you have an empty jar, fill it with whatever you feel is energetically aligned with what you want to manifest at this time. When it's complete—and that may take days or even longer—screw the lid back on and give it to the ancestors, trusting in their desire to help. You might place yours on an altar or bury it; mine went into the Pacific Ocean under starlight.

Give this time. The manifesting jar I created took two weeks of gathering ingredients. I knew a few things that I wanted to go in, but I needed the additional time to make sure every item was in alignment with my intent.

Manifest Casting

Are you still afraid/skeptical/disbelieving that you can manifest? If so, then perhaps you'd like to cast for your manifestation. You'll need a charm casting kit, which includes charms (purchased or DIY), your intent, and a casting board representing the thing you want to manifest. Alternatively—and this is my favorite way to cast—cast charms for each position of whichever tarot spread you're doing. Above all, ask your magical ancestor to help.

I drew three cards: the Ten of Swords, Ace of Pentacles, and the Magician.

I randomly pulled three charms out of the box where my charms live and tossed them onto the spread. A star charm fell on the Ten of Swords, and a turtle and feather both fell on the Ace of Pentacles. Nothing landed on the Magician. Based on the card positions and meanings, how would you interpret the cast?

Interpreting charms can be tricky. This is another of those situations where the best advice is to ask the ancestor for help and then trust the messages you get. Sometimes the answer can seem nonsensical, and that's okay. See if you can find an interpretation that makes sense for you.

Charm casting boards (paper) can be created for almost any purpose, not just manifesting. I've seen some that look like a Ouija board with yes-no-maybe positions. How about a casting sheet with positions for mind-body-spirit-heart? Or you can create something for different facets of your life and magical practice. Don't forget you can also use a chalkboard, which is infinitely changeable. The only limit is your imagination. If you're still a little hazy about a charm casting board and want more ideas, go to *Pinterest.com* and search for charm casting.

Alignment Is a Key

Whether drawing cards, casting charms, or creating manifesting jars, I absolutely guarantee that manifestation is far easier if what you want is in alignment with who you are. For instance, I don't want to manifest a mink coat, as the idea of killing an animal for a coat is abhorrent.

I think we can usually sense if we're in alignment with our highest good, but if you're unsure, I'd like to offer one last manifestation spread, just so you can double-check. Use tarot, an oracle, or Lenormand. Shuffle well, then draw five cards, placing them in a horizontal row.

1. What is my energy around this goal?

2. What about my goal do I most easily align with?

3. What doubts do I need to confront?

4. What magical power do I need to embrace?

5. How can this ancestor help me?

In case you think this doesn't work, let me tell you that this spread kicked my butt. As much as I believe in the power of manifestation, the killer card for me was in position 3—the position of doubt. I drew Justice, which told me that I have doubt that the energy I put into manifesting my goal isn't going to get the return I want—something inside me feels like the scales aren't tipped in my favor. Fortunately, though, the ancestor in position 5 had an invaluable message that got me through the doubt.

Are there positions in your spread that surprised you? Perhaps your alignment is a bit off, or maybe there's not enough energy around your goal to sustain the effort? These are things that need consideration.

Guess What? You Manifested a Gift

Every once in a while, the ancestors drop by to leave a gift. I think it's their way of letting you know they're right alongside you. To discover what gift was left for you by your February ancestor, turn over a single card from any deck you wish.

I drew the Bohemian from the Spirit Oracle. I love this gift because the ancestor is giving me permission to be as unconventional as I want.

That means I can approach manifestation in ways that may seem illogical or nonsensical. I'm all for that.

Daily Draw

February's daily draws are going to focus on manifestation magic. How can you use the symbolism on your morning cards to help you manifest?

One of my cards was the Seven of Wands. In the deck I'm using, this card has two giant bees buzzing around tulips. So of course, I'm going to add a drop of honey to any manifestation jars I'm working on.

Another draw was the Four of Wands. I checked my rune dictionary (Appendix B) to find a rune that I could create with four little sticks. I used Ehwaz, the rune for horse. Works for me.

Which Goddess Are You?

I couldn't leave the time of Brigid without mentioning the Goddess, as I think we've all inherited the blood of one. Regardless of your culture or heritage, some female in your past—perhaps one from the beginning of time—chose to begin a goddess lineage that you are now a part of.

(By the way, if you don't know about Brigid, there's a wonderful book about her listed in Appendix A.)

Some may say that ancestor never existed, but I believe our own ancestral goddess once strode the Earth just as surely as you do today. Let's ask her to reveal herself.

If you happen to own a Goddess deck (Appendix A), you can draw directly from that deck. If you don't have such a deck, go to *Wikipedia.org* and search for "goddesses." Go through the list using your cards or pendulum and find the one that gives you an immediate hit.

I drew from the *Dark Goddess Tarot* and Skadi, the Norse Goddess of Winter and Hunting, appeared. She's all about standing up for what you believe. I couldn't ask for a more precious lineage.

Whom did you find? Who found you?

MARCH

Personal Magic: Healing Magic

March Tools

- ⟐ tarot
- ⟐ pendulum
- ⟐ oracle
- ⟐ finger labyrinth

An Ancestor Who Could Heal

I can't think of a time in history when we needed a Magical Healer more than now.

We can march (a particularly good thing), write government officials (an incredibly good thing), vote (the best ever), and call out abuse when we see it. But what you do best—even if you don't think so—is to embrace your magical gift as a healer of both self and the world. For that, I want to help you connect to an ancestor who could heal, even when working with a world gone blind.

You know, healing isn't only about the body. If you look at various movements during your own lifetime, you can easily find those people whose healing magic and devotion to a cause could change the future: Black Lives Matter and the Keystone XL Pipeline are two that immediately come to mind. Others that are ongoing are Greenpeace (environment), Greta Thunberg (climate), and Majora Carter (urban revitalization). If one little girl sitting outside her school holding a sign about climate change can impact millions, how can that not be magic? The world itself may not be healed because of any of these, but somewhere out there, voices are being heard and healing seeds are planted.

Ready to meet your ancestor?

Separate your deck into Majors, Minors, and Courts. From the sixteen Courts draw a card asking for one of your ancestors—from this bloodline or another life—who practiced magical healing. It's not critical that you know what type of healing they did, as this could range across the spectrum of humankind on Earth. Today we work with systems like Reiki, massage, energy healing, and herbal medicine, but in the distant past, magical healing could have taken the form of touching a wound or calling in the Old Gods to purify the sick.

As you shuffle your Court cards, do it with intent. If you want to tap into an Ancient One, pour that intent into your cards as well.

Who appeared?

After you've drawn your Court card, draw a Major Arcana, asking for what personal healing challenge this ancestor faced. Finally, draw one to three Minor Arcana asking for details about the type of healing they did and how they can help with yours.

Once you've drawn your cards, sit with this ancestor and dialogue via journaling. If needed, ask for more cards that show you *a specific healing skill* that is one of your tools. For example, if you drew the Nine of Wands (the guy with the bandaged head), what would that tell you? For me, this is the Wounded Warrior—the one who can help others battle back from psychological trauma. But that's my interpretation. What's yours?

Still Unsure?

If you don't yet know the area of magical healing for which you're suited, create a pendulum board on which you list the different types of healing you're intuitively drawn to. It could look something like this but use your own words.

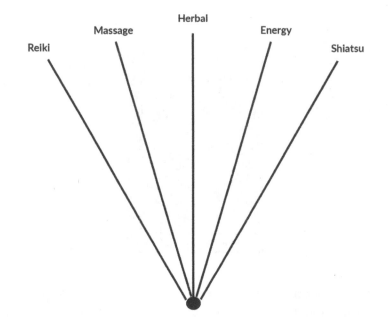

Be sure to ask a clear question and then let your pendulum guide the way. If your pendulum doesn't swing along the lines like the ones I've shown here, just hold it over each of the words. If the pendulum doesn't move at all, this area isn't for you. If it swings a tiny bit, maybe. But if it goes a little wild, you've found the area in which your healing abilities truly are magic. And guess what? It's probably the same area as your magical healer's.

I'll Share This

I asked for an ancestor who could help me improve my distance healing because I work with a group of healers scattered around the globe. The ancestor who appeared was the Queen of Pentacles. When I used my supplementary cards and pendulum, I was told that the Queen was a female, an Ancient One, and had lived in East Africa, around Lake Victoria.

I was half expecting that this ancestor lived in Asia, so I was surprised that I skipped to a different continent.

What about the Queen of Cups' personal healing challenge? I drew Major Arcana 3, the Empress. She wears a crown (royalty), has a shield (warrior), and a dress covered with pomegranates (fertility). She holds an orb (Earth) and is seated in a forest (mystery) through which flows a stream (life). Putting all of this together, you can see how she calmly integrates her own power with that of the natural world.

Depending on the deck you use, she's also generally shown as pregnant. Putting all of that together, I wonder if she worked with pregnant women using medicinal herbs because her own challenge was an inability to have a child. Or she could also have been a natural healer who spoke to the animals, trees, and rivers. It's actually easy to dig deeper into her story using a pendulum.

The Healer's Spread

To learn more about how to work with healing energy, I'm going to introduce you to an unusual spread. It's almost topsy-turvy from how you normally read a tarot spread. To be honest, I hijacked a tiny bit of magic from *The Faeries' Oracle*, which gave me the basis for how it's designed.

The spread begins with *creating a question* that this magical ancestor can help you with. My question was: How can I improve my distance healing magic?

Next, choose any number of cards you'd like (I suggest keeping it between five and nine), then lay them facedown in any order you want. Let your intuition guide you.

My positions looked like this:

```
                                                        7


            2


     1                          5                  4



3


        6
```

Next—and this is the tricky part—decide on the position meanings. This is where the magic really begins, because after you lay the cards, you *now* designate what each position represents. Don't decide on position meanings first. Lay out the pattern, and don't turn the cards over while you're deciding on positions and position meanings.

Your position meanings can be anything *as long as they relate to your question.*

Once you've completed the design and the position meanings, *now* you can turn the cards over and begin your interpretation.

These were the positions I gave my seven cards. (I just heard the number 7 in my head, and that's why I set out a seven-card layout.)

1. Where I am now relative to distance healing?

2. What is my goal in working with this ancestor?

3. What is my past experience as a healer?

4. Where do I hope to be with my healing magic one year from now?

5. What is the Heart of this situation? (This is really the core of my spread.)

6. What are my doubts?

7. What is my ancestral guidance?

After you do the Spread of the Healer, don't you think this would be a good time to stop and transfer everything you've created into your grimoire?

When You Need to Draw an Oracle

As a magical healer, I know you will understand why I'm sharing this story with you.

Here's how this happened. I was working with an ancestor in the usual way—drawing cards from each of my three stacks—and pulled the King of Wands. Since I like fire and action (Wands), I felt a bit of a kinship toward the King—who, by the way, in this instance represented a woman.

When I looked at the challenge of her life by drawing a Major, I got the Hanged Man (12) reversed. The reversal told me that this King had gone through some period of significant sacrifice to arrive at this position. She had gone through a baptism of fire in some way and now life looked oh so different.

I drew another card and got the reversed Four of Swords, another indication that she had gone through something major and now was in a position of finally being healed—or at least renewed.

I wanted to know what in the world had been so traumatic for her, so I went to an oracle deck. The card I drew was called Mother. The card shows a mother bird guarding her nest, except one egg was missing. Looking at the card with the bird keeping guard over the eggs, my guess was that this King lost one of her children.

So now the cards make so much more sense. Can you imagine being the King of action and Fire and knowing that nothing you could do would save your child? It's no wonder that this ancestor was previously the Hanged Man and the Four of Swords.

I think the King did survive in a way, but I'm certain that the period hanging upside down gave her a perspective on life that she wished she never had to see.

How can you use this approach in your healing work? How can you incorporate an oracle deck into your practice?

Why not stop now and do an ancestral healing spread for yourself using two different divination tools?

If your favorite and most perfected healing abilities are in working with plants, use a plant-based oracle. If you are a horse whisperer, find an animal deck. If you heal using specific and customized spells or sigils, begin practicing writing those spells or drawing those sigils.

Are You Too Wounded?

I believe there are some tragedies that are so wounding that getting past them seems impossible. But I also believe your ancestor can give you the tools to at least begin the healing process. If you feel you have suffered traumas that are unhealable, this spread is especially for you.

1. How can my healing begin?

2. What healing skill do I possess?

3. How can this ancestor help me heal?

4. What is my biggest challenge to being healed?

5. What support will I receive from this ancestor going forward?

If you draw a lot of reversed cards, add another question: Why am I drawing so many reversed cards? If you're still unsure about healing, do the following shadow work spread.

Healing within the Shadow

If you're doing shadow work around your healing abilities, shuffle the entire deck and draw three cards. Lay them out in any order.

1. Why do I feel so stuck?

2. What or whom do I blame for the pieces of myself that feel broken?

3. What belief do I hold that doesn't allow me to accept healing?

This spread is one I would journal about, adding imagery that mirrored my feelings around this wound. I know that healing deep pains, especially ones around the family, can feel impossible. Keep working with this ancestor: the solution may not appear today, but my heart hopes it comes soon.

Walking the Way of the Healer

It's estimated that labyrinths have been around for at least three thousand years. If you've never walked one, this is what I can tell you about them: they allow your physical body and your spiritual body to gently collide, resulting in an almost out-of-body healing experience.

It's said that walking a labyrinth is a true healing journey because it can rebalance what has gone askew. I know it sounds kind of mystical, but we're mystical people, right?

The first labyrinth I walked was a portable one. The second was in the country. The third was inside a church, the room aglow in candlelight. The last one was on the grounds of the historic Mission San Luis Rey. Each time I walked, I felt a sense of, well, eternity. When walking a labyrinth, you can allow your mind to cease its chatter and just be.

If you want to walk a labyrinth with an intent to heal, I've included a worldwide labyrinth finder in Appendix A.

In the meantime, did you know that you can "finger walk" a

labyrinth? I know it sounds strange, but if you allow yourself the space and the belief, you'll find a finger labyrinth can be just as powerful as one you actually walk. If the one shown here is not big enough for your finger, enlarge it at a copy shop.

Just note: a labyrinth is not the same as a maze. There is only one way into the center of a labyrinth and one way out. You don't have to worry about getting lost.

Daily Draw

Each day of March that you do a morning or evening draw, think about how it relates to healing. Does it give you a clue about a healing modality? Does it help you understand how you can be healed, either physically or emotionally?

As you spend time with each card, consider if it relates to

⋄ inner child healing   ⋄ grief

⋄ shadow work   ⋄ blocked energy

⋄ chakra healing   ⋄ trauma

⋄ loss   ⋄ anxiety

And always remember: if you're dealing with a physical problem, please see a medical professional.

APRIL

Elemental Magic: Land Magic

April Tools

- ✧ tarot
- ✧ pendulum
- ✧ chakras

The Earth Whisperer

Time to set down roots and immerse ourselves in land magic. Did you know that you have an ancestor who worked with the land in a most magical way? During their own life, the Earth energy they touched reached back and touched theirs.

There have been many books about land energy in both rural and urban areas. There are probably as many that focus on working with nature spirits. This I know: whether farm or city, there are spirits that watch over the land, working in concert with the energy of the land itself. I think, in our busy lives, we tend to walk unthinkingly on top of an Earth that is vibrantly alive with Spirit.

In this, the second month of spring, I invite you to ask for an ancestor who was a land whisperer, an ancestor who knew how to communicate with the nonhuman entities who watch over the land, as well as with the land itself. Although you could work with the energies of the sea and sea-floor, right now let's concentrate on the landmass.

You know, I would typically ask you to draw a Court card or meet this ancestor in the Land of Tarot, but for this month, use whatever form of divination you feel will work best for you.

I went rogue and drew a rune instead—Hagalaz, which I associate with climate crisis, severe weather, or the destructive power of nature. My intuition tells me this ancestor helped Earth to heal after a weather-related catastrophe. Supplementary cards and the pendulum showed this to be an 18th-century woman living in South America.

What system did you use to connect with this ancestor, and what have you learned so far? What can they tell you about working with the spirits of the land upon which you live? What does the land itself have to tell you? Draw as many cards as you like from whatever source you like and begin a conversation.

Don't read on until you've met this ancestor and understand how they worked with land energy.

Although I'll never be a farmer, I do love working with the land—it's a magical skill that I hope you'll embrace as well. But know that if you want to get back to the energies of the land itself, you'll need to bypass the many humans who once lived on the land and work with the nonhuman entities like nature spirits or the fae who are land guardians. Land whispering gives you the opportunity to really broaden your skill set.

Something else to be aware of is that if something of great import happened on the land, it can be reflected in the human spirits who are still hanging around. For example, Joshua Chamberlain, a hero of the American Civil War, upon returning to the battlefield years later said that the bodies disappear but the spirits linger. In other words, a lot of those dead soldiers still inhabit the ground.

That's not to say a battle took place in your backyard, but if you travel back enough years, you can't know what happened there. Remember, you'll encounter nonhuman entities as well as spirits of the dead who have not crossed to the other side.

Working with Land Energy

This spread, meant to be done using tarot, is an introduction to working with the energy of the land. Later, you'll be doing a pendulum exercise that will introduce you to a healing ritual you can do. But for now, let's see what you can learn about your own magical skills and the land where you live.

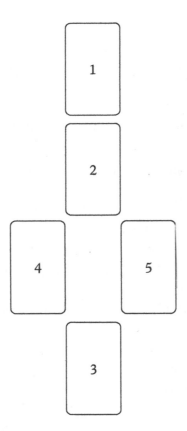

1. My land whisperer skill today

2. My potential in doing land magic

3. How my ancestor can help me connect to land energy

4. How to work with the land guardians

5. A message from the land of my home

When it comes to healing the planet, climate crisis, and extreme weather, we all feel a little puny. But once you begin working with land energy and land guardians, the positive feedback is so quick and filled with such gratitude that you may want to make this a part of your daily practice.

Shadow Work

If you're doing shadow work, draw three cards asking:

1. Do I have preconceived beliefs that obstruct my ability to communicate with land spirits or those who guard the land?

2. Do the land spirits have information that challenges me?

3. What is my right action in working land magic?

The Energy of Your Neighborhood

In the years I've worked with land energy I've found that buildings are often constructed at the exact space two powerful land energies intersect. I'm sure the engineers will tell you the place was chosen for many reasons, but you'll never hear them talk about the energy.

In neighborhood walks I sometimes take a deck of cards or my pendulum and stop where I feel powerful energy. It's an easy way to connect with the land spirits in a place of everyday life.

For practice, try this: draw a simple map of your block.

For my own immediate neighborhood, the two areas of the most noticeable and positive land spirit energy were one house that always plants seasonal, native plants and another house with a small shrine dedicated to their mother. The other places had what I would call neutral energy as the pendulum didn't move at all.

The one thing that did surprise me was holding the pendulum over the place on my hand-drawn map where I live. The pendulum gave a hard tug, almost going up my front walk. Interesting.

Your turn. Whether you want to draw your street, your road, your property, the neighborhood, or just a block, do that now. Then, holding your pendulum over the map, discover both active land spirit energy as well as neutral energy. If you do find active energy, ask if it's positive or negative. Both exist.

As a bonus exercise, if you have casting charms or disks, cast a few on the map. See if they match up with what your pendulum is telling you. If you run into a problem, ask your land whisperer ancestor to help.

Going Deeper

I think one of the most powerful things your magical ancestor can do is to help you understand the land on which you live. To do this you'll need a pendulum and your intuition as well as the ability to visualize.

I've talked a little about land guardians. Trees are an example of a land guardian. Their roots run deep into the earth, and they communicate with other trees—even those at a great distance. They also draw nourishment from the earth and give back healing energy.

It's also possible that you live on land that is watched over by very ancient spirits and is doing very well without your help. Or somewhere in your neighborhood you may find a sad or angry area that needs healing. In my own neighborhood there is a center divide created by river rocks cemented together. They truly hate being trapped in such a way, but all I can do is work with the land and the rock spirits to send them healing, compassion, and love.

If you live anywhere near where a tragic or traumatic event happened, it's possible you'll pick up not only a disturbance in the land but also wandering spirits. Again, work with your own ancestor, asking for protection for you and help with the land.

Next, let's dive into one of the most important practices I can give you for working with your ancestor and the land. If you've forgotten how this ancestor worked their magic, please go back, and reread what you journaled.

I'm going to do this in two parts: first yours, then the land.

Your Chakras

I'm sure you've read plenty about the seven main chakras. They are wheels of energy, and when you're in balance, the wheels spin in a clockwise circle. When you're in an unbalanced state, they can be closed or spin in a counterclockwise direction.

Each chakra is associated with a color and a vibration. These are:

Root (red) located at the base of your spine. This chakra speaks to your need for survival. It's the most primal of all chakras.

Sacral (orange) located below your navel. This is the area of reproduction and creative energy.

Solar plexus (yellow) is in your solar plexus area. This is an area we protect when threatened.

Heart (green) is in the heart area and is associated with love and connections.

Throat (blue) is located at the base of your throat. It relates to communication and expression.

Third eye (indigo) is in the middle of your forehead. This is the chakra of intuition and your sixth sense.

Crown (violet) is atop your head and is your connection to the Divine.

Although you can draw cards for each chakra to get a sense of their state, my preferred method is using a pendulum. Here's how to do this.

Hold your pendulum over a piece of plain paper. Use paper large enough to draw on. Ask the pendulum to "draw" the state of each chakra.

I like using a different colored pencil for each chakra because it shows me at a glance which chakra I'm seeing. The pendulum might go in circles, a straight line, or even make an elongated disk.

If the pendulum swings counterclockwise, it's telling you that chakra is drawing in energy instead of humming along in a nice balanced state. If you see a straight line or an elongated disk shape, there's a blockage there. In this diagram I've numbered each chakra, as you'll see this only in black and white. The little arrows indicate the direction the pendulum was swinging.

Just so you don't have to interpret my messy drawing, chakras 1, 5, 6, and 7 are all working too hard pulling in energy. Chakras 2 and 4 are fine. Chakra 3 is closed.

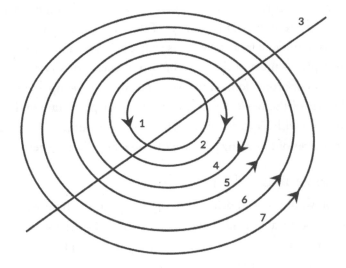

In case you're wondering, the only time I've ever seen seven perfectly round chakras spinning clockwise was when I did a chakra reading on a two-hour-old baby.

I could write a book about using this diagram to work on healing yourself, but instead I want to move on to using this technique in working with the land. After all, that's why we're here.

Land Chakras

Much has been written about the chakras of Earth herself. For many who follow Earth energies, seven points on the planet have been identified for each of the chakras, beginning with the root (Mount Shasta in California) to the crown (Mount Kailash in the Himalayas). But for right now, you're going to work with the chakras of the land under your home. The process is the same as it was for your body. You'll be asking the land to help you understand its current state.

If you do this exercise several times, you'll begin to see energy shifts. If you continue to work with the land, you can see even more drastic shifts. I suggest placing your drawings in your grimoire or drawing directly in the book. Don't forget to time-stamp when you've completed the practice. It's interesting to see shifts related to days of the week or times of day.

The land under a local coffeehouse has a balanced and clockwise spinning solar plexus most of the time, but on weekends it shuts down. This is the chakra of protection; on the weekends there are simply more people than the rest of the week. You'll need to use your pendulum and cards to communicate with the land spirits where you live, but in this case, it was clearly a matter of too many people with too many diverse energies.

To Intervene or Not?

Just as you wouldn't send distant healing to someone who doesn't want it, it's not a good idea to send healing energy to land spirits without asking permission. Sometimes the land is doing just fine without human intervention. I use my pendulum in a yes-no-maybe configuration to ask if the land wants me to help with healing.

If the answer is yes, I then ask if working with chakra colors as a healing medium will work. If that answer is yes, I then send a healing color to the chakra that is most in need. In the case of the coffeehouse, we're talking solar plexus yellow—much like the sun.

If the answer is no, I thank them and move along. If you get a no for color healing, use your pendulum or cards to ask for the appropriate healing modality. Sometimes it's a simple request to pour a cupful of water on the land accompanied by a prayer.

You can see, can't you, that all your tools can work together not only to empower your magical skills but also to help heal this planet? You can thank your ancestor for gifting you this magic.

Daily Draw

Working with a land whisperer is a delight—at least for me. Anytime I feel we humans can have a hand in righting Earth's wounds, I'm all for it.

For your April daily draws, see if you can associate the cards with the energies around where you live or with the ancestor or with your magical work as a land whisperer.

The issues that might arise from your draws could be related to

- Earth healing
- neighborhood hot spots of negative energy
- the energy of the land under your own home
- restless human spirits that need help crossing the veil
- ancient land energies
- tree energy
- ancient land guardians

Always remember to be sure to ask for permission before sending healing energy.

MAY

Celestial Magic: Moon Magic

May Tools

- ⋄ tarot
- ⋄ oracle
- ⋄ message in wax

A Month of Moons

When Galileo Galilei first heard the news out of the Netherlands about a device that made "seeing faraway things as though nearby," he crafted one of his own—a telescope. I have to wonder if, on that May night in 1609, as Jupiter slipped out of the sky, the Italian astronomer realized that in less than a year, he would be the first to see what we now call the four Galilean moons transiting around giant Jupiter.

Using his telescope later in the year, Galileo sketched the features of the moon, finally realizing that the shadows he saw could only have been cast by terrain similar to Earth's: mountains, valleys, and plains. The following year, he published his sketches and conclusions in *Sidereus Nuncius*.

Even before Galileo's lunar observations, humans have been captivated by the golden orb floating in the darkness of space. For centuries across the Earth, cultures have worshipped lunar deities, among them the Zulu iNyanga, Greek Artemis, Roman Luna, Norse Mani, and Hawaiian Lona. In China, the moon is yin, or female, balancing the yang, or male, energy of the sun.

Every month the moon goes from new (dark) to full (fully lit up by the sun). The moon is new when its orbit around Earth places it between the Earth and sun. From our front porch, it looks dark because the illuminated side is facing the sun. We just can't see it.

As the moon continues its movements, more of it becomes visible from Earth when it moves into an orbit that places Earth between the moon and sun. The moon waxes (or grows) until full, then decreases (wanes) back to new. In the Southern Hemisphere the opposite takes place.

Each moon phase has its own energy. Let's explore.

Your Moon Magician

This month, let's call upon an ancestral moon magician. This will probably be one of your most mysterious ancestors, someone whose work was at its most potent after dark.

Separate your deck into Majors, Minors, and Courts. Then use the Court cards to begin this month of lunar receptivity. As you're shuffling your Courts, set an intent not only to meet your moon magician but also that subsequent card draws will help you work with lunar energy.

Draw one card from your Courts, then use your supplementary cards and pendulum to place this ancestor in a specific time and place. If you don't remember how to do that, please refer back to Chapter 5.

Because we perceive the moon as feminine energy, I suggest using a deck that feels more female. This can be a chance for you to employ a totally different deck from your usual one. For me, the *Gaian Tarot* and *Tarot Mucha* feel superfeminine. And while I would rarely use a cat-themed deck for ancestral work, I have one that feels perfect for this work—*Blooming Cat Tarot*.

After you turn over your Court card and have used your pendulum to discover gender, time period, and place for your ancestor, stop for a moment and write down your findings. Think about this. Did your ancestor live before recorded history, at a time when it was common to work with Earth energies and seasonal changes? Or did they live in a bustling place, especially one with a robust male energy like New York City?

Keep in mind that your ancestor's location might give you a more in-depth understanding about why they were called to lunar magic. Intuition and the moon really are best friends. Your ancestor may have lived centuries before artificial light, so seeing the moon and her features clearly would have been far easier than for many of us today.

For my own ancestor, I drew the Queen of Pentacles. This is a female, an Ancient One (I seem to get those a lot), who lived somewhere along what is now the border of France and Germany. Isn't it interesting that my moon magician lived on a border and my cat Queen is sitting on a border between two plants? (See, I told you decks matter . . .)

Queen of Pentacles

Got your card? Good. Before moving on, shuffle the entire deck and draw one card. This represents how working with this ancestor's magic will impact your life.

As an astro-geek, I love lunar astronomy and use a super-detailed moon map. My single card was the Hierophant, which is one of my Birth Pairs so I know that working with lunar energies is part of my life's journey. (Birth Pairs are the two or three tarot cards that are the guiding principles of your life. Briefly, you get to your Birth Pair by adding the numbers of your day, month, and year of birth and then adding the individual digits of the result until you get a single digit or a sum that is 22 or less. For example, if you have a sum of 18, your Birth Pairs are the Moon [18] and the Hermit [9] because 18 reduced to a single number is 9. For more in-depth work with Birth Pairs see my *Ancestral Tarot* or Mary K. Greer's *Archetypal Tarot*.)

Have you drawn your card?

Now, ask your moon magician about their magic. Draw from the entire deck and trust your intuition. You're pulling cards with the intent of discovering *exactly* how they worked with lunar energy and *exactly* how you can do the same. You also want to know if there's a phase of the moon they found particularly potent. Draw as many cards as it takes to get answers to these questions.

You don't have to just use tarot. Ask an oracle, charms, or your pendulum: Was the ancestor a spell maker, smoke diviner, sigil creator, or water healer? Did they draw down the moon—which is drawing the moon's energies into your physical body by envisioning a stream of lunar energy? Maybe they did certain rituals by moonlight, such as harvesting a healing herb or creating a protection symbol. They may have worked with the energy of one complete lunar cycle to plant, propagate, harvest, then lay fallow an act of magic.

If you're wondering how to get all this info via tarot cards, let yourself glide into the card. Ask the other people in the card, draw more cards, use your intuition. I'll show you a quick example.

I asked my Queen of Pentacles for specific information about her moon magic. I drew the Ten of Wands, the Sun reversed, and the Ace of Cups.

The first thing that jumped out at me was the reversed Sun—I immediately heard midnight. The Ace of Cups told me that the new moon was the phase of her most powerful magic. I jumped right into the Ten of Wands because I didn't know why that card appeared. The man put down his wands and spoke to me, saying he was helping build a school of magic—but only in the abstract, and not a physical building. I believe the message was about educating myself more about lunar magic. Lunar work truly is intuitive.

If conversing with a card is a challenge, go back to Chapter 4 and spend some time in the Land of Tarot.

There are no rules here about how many cards you draw or how you interpret them. If any card in a tarot deck speaks to intuition, it's the Moon. The one thing that I do want you to consider, though, is exactly what information you hope to gain from working with this ancestor. Do you want to practice moon magic in the grand sense, or learn how to work with lunar phases? Or is this a type of magic that isn't a good fit for you? Don't just jump into the work if it doesn't feel right.

Now, I wanted to know how I could empower my own moon magic using the energy of a waning gibbous moon, the phase under which I was born. (You can find your own birth moon phase through one of the resources in Appendix A.) This time I drew the Queen of Wands. What I'm hearing through this card is that my moon magic is at its most potent when the sun is in my own sign (Virgo), but just as potent are the days when the moon is in Pisces (Pisces is opposite Virgo in an astrological chart). Just a reminder: the moon changes astrological signs about every two and a half days, which means I can work under a Pisces moon for a few days each month.

The energy of the moon's phases can be used to launch projects (new moon), work on goals, and then feed the energy until the culmination at the full moon. The energy from full to new is a time to gradually release your desires, trusting lunar magic to help you manifest.

Tarot Spreads for the Moon Phases

I originally planned to place each of these moon readings into different chapters, but they wanted to stay together. So be it. The ten spreads following will take you through all the lunar phases as well as introduce you to a Blue Moon and a Black Moon.

How I suggest using this moon magician energy is to do a reading during the appropriate phase of the moon, *regardless of the month you're working in.*

Before each of these readings, draw a single card from the entire deck, asking that month's ancestor for assistance in making the best use—for you—of this phase of the moon. Sometimes they may suggest investing great energy; other times they may recommend letting a phase go and resting. *Let the ancestor lead the way.*

Dark Moon

A dark moon (also called a balsamic moon) is the period just before the sliver of a new moon appears. This is a time of waiting, of stillness, of rest. If you were growing crops, this would be the moon during which to let the soil replenish itself. It's a time for you to replenish yourself.

1. Message of the dark moon

2. Benefit of refraining from working my moon magic

3. How does this time reflect my own Crone state?

New Moon—Set Your Intention

This is a time for fresh starts, clean slates, and planting seeds. Those seeds can be literal or metaphorical. If you pick up a copy of *The Old Farmer's Almanac*, you'll learn the most favorable moon phases for planting a variety of crops. More metaphorical seeds might take the shape of love, money, job, travel, healing, or work.

This New Moon Spread can be done with any divination tool. In fact, if you like, all the spreads in this chapter can be done with decks that are created around lunar energies.

1. Once my intent is set, what is my right action?

2. What seeds can I plant?

3. What are my hidden beliefs that challenge my intent?

4. What hard truth do I need to hear?

5. How do I hold space for my intent?

Waxing Crescent—The Seeds Are Planted

The waxing crescent is a time of clarifying intention, being hopeful, and envisioning the seeds you planted at the new moon taking root. This is a time when lunar energy is building, so be careful what energies you're pouring into your goal. Doubt will cloud your success.

1. What small seeds are beginning to take root?

2. What fertilizer is needed at this time?

3. How can I use my personal moon magic at this time?

4. How do I stay focused?

First Quarter and Third Quarter—Balance

During first and third quarter, the moon is equally in light and darkness. In first quarter the right side of the moon is lit; at the third quarter, it is the left side. (Do this spread on both phases.)

This is a time when lunar energy is seeking balance, whether growing or fading. If you don't see your goal beginning to manifest by the first quarter, do this spread and look for subtler signs in sidewalk oracles or omens. If you've having trouble releasing during the third quarter, use an oracle to find out the appropriate action.

1. Where is my intent in balance?

2. Where is my intent out of balance?

Waxing Gibbous—Almost There

Most of the moon is now in lit by the sun. Now is the time to review your goals and reevaluate the steps you've taken. This is the phase that correlates to standing in the doorway just before you take the first steps into a room. You are on the verge of a successful culmination of your goal. Be watchful during this time as the energies can speed up as they close in on the full moon.

1. What is the last-minute challenge to my success?

2. How do I counter that challenge?

Full Moon—It's Finally Happening

The promise of your intent has been met. This is the most powerful time for the Mother energy of the Triple Goddesses. Be grateful, acknowledge your gratitude, and give back to your community, friends, family, or those in need. I also see this as a time to honor the ancestor who stepped forward this month. What can you do to honor them?

1. What motivated this goal?

2. How do I activate the energy I've built up?

3. What is the nature of my success?

4. How can I expand my success?

5. How can I navigate successfully to the next phase?

If your intended goal has not been met during this moon phase, draw cards to answer two questions:

1. Is this an intent that, by its nature, needs to grow over several more phases?
2. Is this an intent that isn't for my highest good?

Waning Gibbous—Slowly Fading

Harvest your crop; release the energy that you've been building since the waxing crescent. Resolve any lingering doubts, challenges, or conflicts relating to your goal during this lunar cycle.

1. What full moon energy remains?
2. What full moon energy is rapidly decreasing?
3. What is my right action?

Almost Gone—Waning Crescent

This is the final phase in the lunar cycle. Just because the full moon energy has faded does not mean this is a time of powerlessness. In fact, the opposite is true. Your moon magician worked in darkness. Now is the time for you to do the same, preparing for the dark moon.

1. What energy needs to be released?
2. What energy needs to be saved for another moon cycle?

Two Additional Moons

There are two more moons you can experience, both with powerful energies. One is the blue moon. This is the second full moon in a month. Imagine working with your lunar cycle through two full moons and you'll get an idea of the magic of a blue moon.

The second type of moon is called a black moon. This is a rare occasion when there are two new moons in a calendar month. Equally as powerful as a blue moon, a black moon invites you into periods of stillness and reflection.

BLUE MOON MAGIC

1. My lunar shadow (limiting beliefs)

2. How does my lunar shadow manifest in my life?

3. How do I break free from my lunar shadow?

BLACK MOON MAGIC

1. What worries am I carrying?

2. What can I do to wipe those worries away?

3. What is the outcome of a clean slate?

A Moon Message

You've always had the power, my dear, you just had to learn it for yourself.

—GLINDA THE GOOD WITCH (*THE WIZARD OF OZ*)

Interpreting moon messages, sidewalk oracles, or omens is always a case of trusting your intuition. And, as Glinda said, you've always had the power to do it. This is an exercise that I personally would do under my birth moon phase or a dark moon. It is a practice of asking your moon magician for a message.

There's no need for tarot cards, runes, oracles, or a pendulum. But you will need:

- melted wax
- a container of water

Years ago, I was fascinated by a psychic who read wax instead of cards. I've always loved this practice, particularly when I can ask the ancestors for a message.

Unless you're using drippings from a candle, be supercareful with melting block wax. It can catch on fire, so use a throwaway pan that you can employ as a double boiler.

You can melt a block of wax, but using melted wax from a candle is much easier. Here's how to receive your ancestral moon message.

Light a candle with intention and let the wax melt into a glass of water. If you want a message about a specific question, choose a candle of the appropriate color:

- red—courage
- white—new beginnings
- pink—love
- green—money, success
- blue—communication
- purple—intuition
- black—protection
- yellow—intelligence

After lighting your candle, allow it to drip wax into your water until you *feel* you have enough wax drippings. Give it a bit of time and then pull the wax out of the water. Now, you'll interpret the shape relative to your intent or question. Yes, it's as simple as that.

If you've never done this before, wax that's hardened in water can take on the most fantastic shapes. Sometimes mine look like a Martian city; other times like a series of mysterious tunnels. Whatever shape your wax forms, use it to answer the question you asked the ancestor.

Moon in the Signs

Just as lunar energy shifts during moon cycles, so too is it affected by the astrological sign the moon is moving through. Here's a bird's-eye view of the moon through the signs:

Aries—Pedal to the metal. Get started.

Taurus—Focus on values, possessions.

Gemini—Variety, quick movement

Cancer—Compassion, nurturing

Leo—Self-expression, creativity

Virgo—Work, health

Libra—Partnerships, art

Scorpio—Psychic, ambition

Sagittarius—Exploration, travel

Capricorn—Recognition, commitment

Aquarius—Ideas, the future

Pisces—Dreams, mysticism

Daily Draw

May is a wonderful month to communicate with your ancestor. Although I typically draw cards in the morning, during this month my draws are going to come under moonlight. There are so many questions to ask during lunar cycles, but I suggest asking the questions that relate to the energy of a specific moon phase.

Questions could include:

- ⁘ What should I focus on during this lunar cycle?
- ⁘ What have I released?
- ⁘ What do I want to grow?
- ⁘ What needs my energy at this time?
- ⁘ What is holding me back?
- ⁘ What needs cultivating?
- ⁘ What can no longer stay hidden?

Remember to include your moon magic ancestor while working with lunar phases. They like being a part of your magic.

JUNE

Celestial Magic: Solstice Magic

June Tools

- ✧ tarot
- ✧ sigils
- ✧ altar

Here Comes the Sun

In this month of the summer solstice, use the energy of the sun to practice whichever form of magic you feel most drawn to. The solstice is a time to honor the sun. Without it, no life can exist on Earth. Without the sun Earth would be a frozen rock tumbling in space. We need the sun to grow crops, which, in turn, feed us and the animals.

Ancient civilizations often built dwellings facing south so they could capture both light and heat. In countries with an abundance of sun but little fuel, year-round cooking is possible via solar cookers. Solar panels can produce electricity, and solar cells can power satellites.

For people who suffer from seasonal affective disorder (SAD), sunlight is the difference between having a day of energy or a day of depression. The sun is also our main source of vitamin D production, which comes through the simple process of sunlight falling on our skin.

Work with your magical skills in conjunction with the sun and you'll have created your own nuclear power plant.

Your Solstice Magician

Because solstice energy is so powerful, this month you're going to connect with your ancestor using one of the twenty-two Major Arcana. Pull one Major at random, asking for an ancestor who worked with solar energy. Since you are merging your work with the sun, you can focus on *any magical skill you choose.*

Do you want to become an evidentiary channeler? Do you want to create art that heals? Build a home that's in sync with nature? Or do you want the ultimate magic of helping those preparing to cross over into the Ancestral Realm? This is *the* best time of the year to bring big dreams, big hopes, big magic into being.

Now is a perfect time to ask for a magical ancestor who could change their world by working solstice magic. This may be one of your most powerful ancestors, so don't be afraid to ask for the magic you're called to live. Dream the dream that's big enough.

Which card did you pull and how do you relate this to your solstice magician?

I drew the Strength card (8) and immediately thought about trees—the ones with both deep and shallow roots. Where I live it's common to see ficus roots cracking sidewalks because they run along the top of the ground. But the tree I saw with Strength was an oak with roots that grew so deep that even the most destructive tornado or hurricane would leave it untouched. That's the ancestor who came to me. Clearly, they used their magic in conjunction with the sun to work with nature.

Once you've drawn your card, what do you think about it? Do you get an immediate hit about this ancestor, or do you need time to ponder it? If you want to know more, draw other cards (from the Minors) asking questions like:

- ⟡ What was your life like?

- ⟡ How do I strengthen my connection with you?

- ⟡ What am I overthinking about magic?

- ⟡ How can you help my wounded self accept my magic?

- ⟡ What was the nature of your magical work?

Use tarot, an oracle, or runes in dialogue with this ancestor.

Did you take the time to draw supplementary cards or use your pendulum? Honestly, I was shocked to discover my ancestor was a male who lived in 20th-century North America. Once I got that information, I knew exactly who it was and why he was coming through. If you haven't done this process, take a moment and see if someone you knew is coming forward. If not, who has appeared?

After this, draw one more card—this time from the Courts. The question to ask your ancestor for this card is: What was your energetic vibration?

It was no surprise that the vibration of my Strength ancestor was the Knight of Cups, as it's a card I've drawn time and again and makes total sense given the fact that I know who this was.

After you find your ancestor, work with them throughout the month. Don't just draw and forget the ancestor. They're coming into your life for a specific reason. Take the time to discover exactly why. Honor their connection and commitment to you.

How to Work with Your Solar Ancestor

If you've been reading along since January, you'll know that I'm not keen on ambiguous answers. This spread, which you can do using either tarot or an oracle deck, should give you specific answers. If it doesn't, draw cards to clarify.

1. What is my most potent magic at this solstice?

2. What is my biggest challenge to stepping into my power?

3. Exactly what magic did my ancestor practice?

4. How can my ancestor help in my practice?

5. What magic is the solstice bringing into my life?

6. How can I honor and thank this ancestor?

May I share just one of my own cards? The challenge to my path in position 2 was the Moon. This Virgo likes to have a map of the journey, and the Moon's message is this: *that map does not exist nor will it ever.* My challenge is to live with the unknown and to keep moving forward even if I have no idea where that journey will lead.

I think right now is a great time to stop and ask you to look at all the cards you've drawn. If you used tarot, are there missing suits? Is there a preponderance of one suit? Are there multiple Court cards or Major Arcana? Consider not only the six cards of this spread but also the ones drawn for your ancestor.

I drew more Major Arcana than is mathematically logical, and almost two-thirds of my cards were Wands. For me, Wands are solar power (Fire) and have an obvious relationship to my own star magic. Remember, stars are pretty much just big nuclear furnaces.

I'm so curious about your cards and what you've learned. Feel free to email me with what you've discovered.

A Solstice Sigil

What is the magic you can merge with solstice energy? Once you know what that is, take the time to create a solstice sigil—one that represents the most powerful magic that lives within your own solar engine.

Use the Square Method from Chapter 5. If working in some magical fashion with family patterns is your sweet spot, you may want to use the word *family*. If so, your sigil would look like this:

Refresher: Family = 6-1-4-9-3-7. The sigil begins in the 6 square and ends in 7 square.

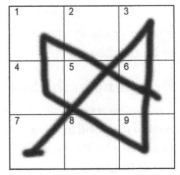

Creating your sigil with intent is the first part of the process. Activating it is the second. In this season of the solstice, what can you do to activate your sigil? You could:

- ⁘ make it part of a spell
- ⁘ leave it outdoors or in a window for an entire solar day (twenty-four hours)
- ⁘ place the sigil under a yellow candle, as yellow is associated with Apollo, the Greek and Roman god of the sun
- ⁘ carve it into a piece of yellow fruit and then eat it or leave it outdoors as an offering
- ⁘ place it on your altar or workspace

This is one sigil I would not put under my pillow, as my goal is to energize my solstice magic—that wouldn't make for great sleep.

Another choice is leaving your sigil out in nature and letting the elements do with it as they will. This is the ultimate release.

Build an Outdoor Solstice Altar

Building an outdoor solstice altar space is easy, as the only materials you'll need are what you find on the ground. My materials were a collection of leaves and seedpods, arranged in a sunlike circle. The pods marked the cardinal directions while the leaves formed the circle.

What I loved most about this solstice altar is that the wind and weather gradually unbuilt the design, scattering the leaves and pods back to Mother Nature.

Breathing in the Sun

Your ancestors carefully tracked the solstices and equinoxes and built sites around the world in alignment with the sun at solstice. Just a few are Stonehenge, Machu Picchu, and Chaco Canyon.

This month—and you don't need to wait for the solstice—begin weaving the practice of Breathing in the Sun into your own magical skills. I think you'll find this enhances whatever form of magic you've chosen to work with. You can do this at any time, as breathing in the sun is akin to breathing in a new day.

The Process

Face east and breathe in and out four times, consciously breathing in the energy of the sun. It doesn't matter if you can see the sun, just place yourself in alignment with where it's rising. If you don't know where the sun is rising this month or if you don't know directions, get one of the astronomical apps from Appendix A and search for the sun. The app will point the way.

Next, turn ninety degrees to your right and repeat your four deep breaths, breathing in the sun's energy. Next, turn ninety more degrees right and repeat, then once more and repeat. Then turn ninety more degrees and you're back facing east.

Now, repeat the process but make your ninety-degree turns to the left.

Doing this with closed eyes is the standard way, but if that makes you feel off balance, you may keep your eyes open.

If you want to add additional layers to this practice—and I usually do—as you face each direction, give thanks to the energy of both the sun and the direction. When I do this practice, it is never the same. Sometimes at one direction I hear the names of animals, at others I'm simply being asked to be grateful. I think the most startling thing I've experienced is Breathing in the Sun and then, when I open my eyes, seeing the room as if I were sitting on the ceiling. What a surprise!

This is a powerful exercise and one that you might want to do with your ancestor at your side. I'm certain you'll be divinely guided.

Daily Draw

I think the most important thing I can tell you about June's daily draws is to allow the cards and your ancestor to help you in increasing your magical abilities utilizing the power of the summer solstice.

Possible topics:

- future magical skills
- further work with solar energy
- hidden skills that need developing
- how to keep growing my skills
- overcoming my shadow (fears)

As an example, what if your daily draw is the Page of Swords? What message do you think he has around this month's focus? Solstice happens when the sun "stands still," just as this Page is doing. Do you need to stop on this day, reassess, ask for bird omens, or sharpen your magical skills?

JULY

Elemental Magic: Weather Magic

July Tools

- ⟡ tarot
- ⟡ bull-roarer
- ⟡ rainstick

Working with Weather Magic

Each of your family lines has different skills. This month let's see if there's a weatherman in your family. If so, was this ancestor from your dad's side or your mom's? Let's see.

Divide your deck into Majors, Minors, and Courts. Then draw one card from each pile for your mom's side of the family and one from each pile for your dad's side.

Place the two lines of three cards so you can see both at the same time.

For example, my mom's magical family line appeared as the King of Swords, the Moon reversed, and the Seven of Wands.

My dad's magical family line showed up as the King of Cups, the Hanged Man reversed, and the Five of Cups reversed.

After you've drawn your cards, pick the family line that you think the weather magician was born into. You may have a tough time deciding. If you're torn, journal about each of the cards; often something will occur to you while you are making notes about your draws.

In the end, I chose to work with an ancestor on my dad's side since the King of Cups is a Water card, as is the Five of Cups. Interestingly, the Hanged Man is associated with Water and the planet Neptune. With three watery cards, that feels very weather-y to me.

I'm really interested in doing weather magic because I know magical weather played a part in some important events in American history and I've always hoped one of my weather magicians was part of it. (By the way, you'll find magical interventions of all sorts once you start digging into history. For my UK friends, you might tap into those who called up a shield of protection over your country during World War II. If you don't know what I'm referring to, google Dion Fortune and WWII.)

Use your supplementary cards and pendulum to learn more. Don't be surprised if the answers are unexpected ones. For example, although I want to know about early American weather workers, it's possible my ancestor lived centuries before America was even a thing.

What Have You Learned So Far?

1. Did you choose a family line and journal your notes?

2. Which Court card did you draw?

3. After drawing your Major and Minor Arcana cards, what have you learned about the kind of magic this ancestor practiced? Were they focused on rain, snow, wind, ocean waves?

4. How many generations of magical weather workers are in your lineage? You should ask. Then draw cards, journal, and, above all, trust your intuition.

5. What is the most important act of weather magic your ancestor performed?

For instance, when I asked about magical ancestors in early America, I drew the Ten of Wands. I'm all for keeping things simple, so I'll accept that ten people in my own bloodline worked with weather in a magical way and they lived in the early days of the country.

Next, I wanted an inkling of the kind of magic they practiced. I drew ten cards—one for each person—and turned up six Cups, two Pentacles, one Sword, and one Wand. I'd say the preponderance of Cups is telling me that some form of water was part of their magical practices. As I write this, I'm hearing that those six all belonged to the same family—grandparents, parents, and children.

For you, this may not be an interesting or exciting form of magic. But once you begin to dig into various forms of ancestral magic, I think you'll understand the value of keeping connected to this ancestor. If you're still hazy about the type of weather magic, get your pendulum and create a divining board of a piece of paper on which you've written the types of weather magic. You don't even have to draw lines on this one. Just hold your pendulum over each word and see what happens. If you get nothing, then weather may not be for you. If your pendulum moves, you now have a starting place. As this is part of your own lineage, it's something that you're innately good at, even if you don't know it now.

The suit of your Court card will tell you about the energy of the magic. For example, Swords are all about Air, so probably cloud movements, storm clouds, rain, and snow. If you got Cups, it was probably ocean or river magic. Pentacles most likely relate to any weather that has to do with crops. Wands are about Fire. Lightning strikes create forest fires and have for as long as there have been weather and forests. Although we hate to see a fire, sometimes it's needed for new growth. What other types of weather magic do you relate to Wands?

Since ten people in my family line were involved in some type of water-related weather magic, I'm digging a little deeper. If you have water workers, they may have worked with weather and water as scryers, shell diviners, or those who used water to heal.

Weather Magic of July

It's funny but not surprising that the Hanged Man correlates with the planet Neptune, and in July the Romans celebrated Neptunalia, a festival for the god of the sea. I guess our ancient Roman ancestors wanted a way of conjuring rain on a sizzling summer day just as much as we do.

You've probably never heard of an old movie called *The Rainmaker*. In it, Burt Lancaster is a con artist who convinces a drought-stricken Kansas town to pay him to make it rain. I'll spare you the whole story, but in the end (spoiler) the con man falls in love and manages to—miraculously—make it rain.

So, because I'm a history geek, I want to tell you my favorite magical weather story. During the War of 1812, the British set fire to Washington, D.C. (I forgive you, my UK cousins.) With fires raging, out of nowhere came a tornado followed by a violent and torrential rain. There were even reports of a hurricane. Poof! No more fire. Now that's some weather magic.

I have one more story, and this one I witnessed. (Actually, I may have witnessed the 1812 one, too.) During a few extremely hot and dry months when we desperately needed rain, my sister took a bull-roarer out to the garden and called in the rain. If you've never heard one of these things, it creates a low pitched moan that can be heard over a great distance. I guess some ancestral weather worker heard it because in a couple of days it rained.

If you're interested in weather magic, start with a little rainmaking. You can make your own bull-roarer out of wood and string or buy one online.

But bull-roarers aren't the only thing that can bring rain. The fae are quite good at weather work as well. Although they don't really have a place here in an ancestral magic book, I'm certain many of your ancestors worked magic with the faeries.

I also want to mention rainsticks. The ones I have worked with were made from a dead cactus filled with small pebbles—and with the nasty thorns hammered inside. But you can easily make your own rainstick with things you have around the house.

DIY Rainsticks

You'll need:

> empty paper towel tube
>
> tiny nails (like tacks)

packing tape

beans or tiny pebbles

rice (alternative)

foil (alternative)

This is a simple and fantastic way to get into weather magic. Push little tacks in a random pattern into an empty paper towel tube. Tape one end of the tube shut with packing tape, pour in beans, small pebbles, or rice, then tape the other end shut. Of course, you'll want to make it pretty—perhaps you could paint it blue with raindrops of white?

Alternatively, you can ditch the tacks and instead line the inside of the paper towel roll with foil. Then add the rice and plug up the ends.

To use, simply turn your rainstick end over end and you'll hear the sound of rain.

Since I live in the arid Southwest, rainmaking is one of the more appealing weather magic skills I'd like to improve. How about you?

Whistling Up the Wind

Rainmaking isn't the only kind of weather magic there is. I don't want to leave July without talking about whistling up the wind. There have been tales throughout history of weather workers who have destroyed a rival's crops or sunk a ship, but that stuff isn't for us. Still, if you're serious about improving or learning this skill, let's talk about whistling up the wind. In places where it's hot and dry and the air is still, it's so refreshing if a wind comes up. I think we've all been there.

The technique for wind whistling is simple. First, focus on what you want to achieve, then draw in a deep breath, allowing the energy of your breath to merge with that of wind magic and your intent. Next, blow the breath out in the form of a whistle. If you can't whistle, then blow the breath out into a bottle to produce a whistle. You can also make a little wind whistle if you can get your hands on a piece of wood that you can hollow out.

This takes some time, practice, and focus, but it's something you can do, even if weather magic isn't part of your lineage. Try it. And let me know how it goes.

Weather Omens

Since our ancestors were mostly farmers before the Industrial Revolution, the weather was of immense importance. I suppose that's why so many legends, myths, and sayings have sprung up around weather. How many of these have you heard?

Red sky at night, sailors' delight; red sky at morning sailors take warning.

As the day grows longer, the cold grows stronger.

When the bees crowd out of their hive, the weather makes it good to be alive. When the bees crowd into their hive again, it is a sign of thunder and of rain.

If the groundhog sees his shadow on February 2, winter will last six more weeks.

Rain, rain, go away, come again some other day.

When dew is on the grass, rain will never come to pass.

If there's a ring around the moon, expect rain or snow soon.

If spiders are spinning their webs, look for dry weather ahead.

When the wind is in the east, it's good for neither man nor beast. When the wind is in the north, the old folk should not venture forth. When the wind is in the south, it blows the bait in the fishes' mouth. When the wind is in the west, it is of all the winds the best.

It's just something to think about.

Daily Draw

Every morning in July my draws focused on water because that's what I want to practice. I suggest you do something similar with your draws and your weather magic.

Draw a card a day. If you know your weather magic, consider how each of those cards can be a guidepost to your own practice.

Since I'm concentrating on water, I pay particular attention to the Cups cards as well as the Court cards and Major Arcana associated with water. I drew the Seven of Cups and this prompted me to get out seven cups of my own, fill them with water, and see if I could read any images in the water. Water scrying is not one of my skills. But, I keep trying.

AUGUST

Personal Magic: Past Life Magic

August Tools

- ❖ tarot
- ❖ rattle
- ❖ bindrunes
- ❖ crystals

Dipping into the Past

Whether you once sailed with Vikings or galloped across the grasslands of Eurasia a thousand years ago, you, too, have walked this Earth before. And even though you may not know it, a lifetime of yours is still rattling around today. Just because you're living in a modern age doesn't mean a pattern from another life isn't lurking in the corner, repeating itself time and again.

If you've never worked with past lives, I want to tell you why I think the work is valuable. Almost everyone I know has felt at home somewhere they've never lived or even visited. My sister's place is on the Northern Plains of Wyoming; mine are many, including the ancient Southwest. We don't remember those places unless they're important to our life today. That's because we still carry the memories, talents, likes, and dislikes, as well as the pains and disappointments from those times to now.

Are you willing to visit the Land of Tarot this month? If you can't remember the way, travel back to Chapter 4. While there, ask to meet an ancestor from a time when the two of you were bound by blood. This is the ancestor who's going to help you identify a life that has left a troublesome pattern that is plaguing you even today. They will appear as a Court card.

If visualizing the Land of Tarot just doesn't work for you, then go ahead and draw a card from the Courts.

Once you've connected with your ancestor, use your supplementary cards and pendulum to locate them in a time and place. You might get a quick hit, or you may need to draw additional Major, Court, and Minor cards until you're receiving a clear signal. Please don't move forward until you know what life you shared with this ancestor.

The more specific a life you can identify, the more meaningful the rest of your past life work will be.

Here's a short example. The ancestor who rode up to me in the Land of Tarot was the Knight of Pentacles. The Knight was a woman who lived in 17th-century southern France. You know, the very first thing that came to mind for me is that this was the peak period of witch trials in Europe. (Let your intuition out of the box, okay?) Of course, I went searching online and found the Labourd (France) witch-hunt of 1609, in which seventy people were executed. I know without drawing more cards that this is the life the Knight and I shared.

Here's where I'd like you to really dig into the cards and pull out more specifics. Think of yourself as an evidentiary channeler, and see if you can find factual information in your cards or at least enough detail for you to identify any remaining trauma, wounds, or patterns from that life. (If you don't know about evidentiary channeling, it's channeling that produces provable facts.)

Next, use any divination tool you choose to do this spread.

1. A trait from the identified past life that I'm repeating today
2. An unresolved family issue from that life
3. Past life family pattern to embrace
4. Past life family pattern to banish
5. Why is this life so important for me to remember?

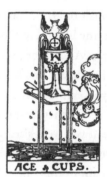

I drew the Lovers, the Ace of Cups, the Emperor, the Five of Swords, and the Devil. Without even getting into each card individually, I know this was a significant life because out of five cards, three were Major Arcana. This would indicate major life lessons—and not only then but also now. Missing are cards from the Pentacles and Wands suits, although the

Emperor correlates to Aries (Wands) and the Devil to Capricorn (Pentacles). So, in a way, all suits are represented.

I think position 5 is a critical card because it's telling me—quite bluntly—why it's so important to tap into this lifetime. Do you notice that the first card and the last (Lovers and Devil) mirror one another? There's a story in those two cards, believe me.

But for now, what do you do about the information you've just received? Select the cards you feel are most important to work with *at this time*. For me, it's position 4: the family pattern to banish. I know exactly what this means in my life today. Do you know which of your cards are the ones to tackle first? And, after journaling, do you understand why this past life is such an important one for you to remember?

As you can tell, this is more than a simple five-card spread. Each of the cards can generate question after question along with more cards and clarifiers. If you were sitting across from me right now and these were your cards, we'd delve into that Five of Swords from your past life and how it's causing pain in this one. There are so many questions to ask; fortunately, you have the tools to find the answers.

Going Back a Little Further

Throughout the book are references to past lives. Many of us have experienced either déjà vu or a sense of being home, although far from home. While I can't prove past lives (unless I get far better at evidentiary mediumship), I can say that I know for certain that I've been here before, in other times and other guises.

Past lives are a key component of ancestral work. When identifying family patterns, it's hard to differentiate between a pattern that began with your great-great-grandparents or one from another lifetime. For me personally, the latter are much more personal patterns than familial. That means those lives have stayed with me throughout time and one day or another I need to embrace or banish them.

I think we all know how to embrace a pattern. For example, I happily embrace my family's love of music and of playing musical instruments. Music is a healer. In fact, in my dad's line a family from 300 years ago moved from one town to another because they were so enchanted by the new town's music.

But how about banishing a pattern? If a form of abusiveness has followed you throughout lifetimes, what do you do about it? Keeping silent about an abusive or toxic family is a killer. Trying to fight it from the inside out alone is a road I don't suggest or envy.

If the toxic pattern is bleeding so much into your life that it's hard to be truly functional, working with a medical professional can be the difference between living in the dark and turning on a light.

In conjunction with that professional work, you may want to explore right action by using divination tools. In some cases, an outright banishing spell might be called for. You'll find lots of suggestions online, but the path I choose—because it suits who I am—is more about forgiveness. I know this can be one of the most difficult things you'll ever say about an abusive or toxic pattern or person, but it's one I've found to be magically effective.

I hold the situation or person in my mind, and out loud I repeat these words: "I love you, I bless you, I release you. I breathe in truth, I breath out not truth."

Trust me, I know that you may choke on the "I love you" part, as I have. But I also know that cruelty is often the weapon of a wounded soul. As a healer, this is how I work. As a magical person you may choose a different path.

For some, banishing the toxic pattern from other lifetimes may take the form of writing a letter to that pattern and burning it. If you place all your feelings about the toxicity into the paper and into the words, this can be a powerful way to release the pattern. Please use a big enough container when burning the paper—I've seen flames leap almost a foot high out of a bowl that's filled with toxicity.

You can also create a small doll that is stuffed with paper on which you've written all your anger, regrets, resentments, and even hatred. Once complete, throw the doll away, preferably somewhere far from where you live. Before tossing it, repeat "I banish you"—and mean it.

Get Specifics

I'm sure by now you've identified a significant past life. Hopefully you have a sense of the big picture of that life, but if not, do this nine-card spread to get into the specifics. Use the entire deck or an oracle deck if you choose.

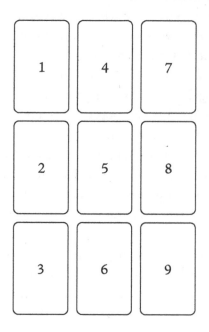

1. Who was I?

2. My life path in that past life

3. The essence of that incarnation

4. The most important lesson I learned

5. My biggest challenge in that life

6. My most important success

7. What I wish I had done differently

8. Who is with me today from that life?

9. Message from my past life me to the me today

It took me several hours of back-and-forth journaling and thinking before I could wrap my head around the cards I drew. But the time is so worth it because this was a life from which I'm now repeating a troublesome pattern. It's time to put it to bed.

I would love to know what you discover . . .

Rattling the Divine

In some cultures, rattles are associated with the supernatural. For me, they're a way of calling in ancestors from other lives. That's because there are days I don't want to use any kind of oracle. Instead, I want the energy of the rattle.

If you would like to connect with a past life ancestor this way, let me show you how to make and use one.

I make my rattles using locally sourced gourds, feathers, a piece of branch, and a bit of leather. But the magic, itself, is not the rattle. It's the intent you have while collecting the pieces to make the rattle, as well as the energy of what goes in it. Because of the power you're building within the rattle, don't share your personal ingredients.

You'll need:

An empty gourd

A stick for a handle

Some leather or feathers for decoration

A tool to make a hole in the gourd for the handle

The magical ingredients: Although the ingredients of my most powerful rattle are secret, I can tell you that in some of the rattles

I've made I've included cherry pits—just as some Native Americans had done before me. Some were combinations of feathers, crystals, seeds. In other words, I consider whatever energy I want to create. When you make your rattle, fill it with objects that contain the energy of your intent.

Calling in ancestors from another life is only one way to use a rattle. If you do distance healing (refer to March), hold the person's image in your mind while rattling for their highest good. The energy created from rattling is hard to describe, other than to say that you will probably feel it somewhere around your crown chakra.

What if you made a rattle for *you*, either as a tool of healing or divination or calling in the Beloved Dead? What would you put inside it? How about a sprig of rosemary for remembrance and bloodstones for family?

If you decide to make one for this specific past life ancestor, you might draw a card asking for the most appropriate energy. For instance, I drew the Knight of Swords, which tells me that the magical ingredients would need to feel swift and a little erratic.

After completing your rattle, begin to use it before your morning draw or when doing healing on yourself or others. Rattle energy can be incorporated into any of your magical practices. It will add tenfold energy to whatever you do.

Reaping from Another Life

The days of August mark the last of summer. This is the time your past life ancestors—and you—would have started bringing in crops for the coming cold weather. In Western culture of centuries ago, this was the time of the harvest.

In both the Northern and Southern Hemispheres, August was a time of reaping. In the north, it was for wheat and potatoes; in the south, the crops of spring. But that's just about things you would have grown. What about other types of harvest? What have you sown so far this year that you can reap during the first harvest of August? And how do the crops you bring in relate to your past life?

The Harvest Spread

Shuffle your entire deck—either tarot or oracle—and draw five cards. Consider each card as it relates to your life today. Be sure to write down your draws because, once your draw is complete and the cards go back in the deck, a day from now they will vanish from your memory. These cards represent the harvest of the lifetime you've been working with this month.

1. What am I in the process of harvesting?

2. What needs more time to grow?

3. What seed never took root?

4. A card for clarification (any deck, rune, or charm)

5. A card for meditation

Don't forget that you're working with this past life ancestor all month—so call on them if you need help understanding your cards.

How do the cards from the past and now compare? Did you get any of the same cards in the past life and this life?

In my past life, the seed that never took root was Death reversed. I believe that relates to my inability in that life to walk between worlds.

Protecting the Home and Family

Since we're spending time in another life, do you remember a life when you carved or painted symbols in your home for protection? The life you lived could have been in any century, but you understood the need to stay safe, regardless of when you lived. Even today, there are protective hex signs painted or hung on Pennsylvania Dutch barns. See, we aren't that far away from our past lives, are we? Old habits die hard.

If you feel drawn to take a page from another life, create a bindrune for protection. It could be one to protect your home, your children, your magical practice, or even your animals.

Bindrunes are a combination of two or more runes, created for a specific purpose. For now, you'll be creating one for protection—although if another intent calls to you, heed the message. You'll find the runic alphabet in Appendix B.

Choose the runes that, for you, best represent protection of home and family. For me, the runes that best fit my needs are Othala (heritage) and Gebo (gift). My bindrune combines both, asking Spirit to protect my gift of the ancestors.

It's okay to add multiple runes together. For example, you may want to include runes for prosperity.

By the way, you can find a link to an automatic bindrune maker in Appendix A.

A Past Life Gift

I couldn't leave August without asking your past life ancestor for a gift to help on your journey. This is a simple one-card draw. Before drawing, perhaps offer a prayer of gratitude?

My gift was the Page of Pentacles. It's to remind me that it can take lifetimes to change deeply ingrained patterns. But they assure me, change is always in the wind.

Daily Draw

Instead of August daily draw suggestions, I'm going to ask that you do this reading for yourself and your ancestor *in the life you shared.* You may use whatever form of divination you choose. If you pick an oracle or tarot, the questions to draw for are:

1. What was our life like growing up?

2. What kind of work did I do?

3. What was my life purpose?

4. What is it I wanted more than anything else?

5. Overall, my life was _____.

6. As I left this life, I thought about _____.

SEPTEMBER

Celestial Magic: Sky Magic

September Tools

- ⋅⋅ tarot
- ⋅⋅ crystals
- ⋅⋅ finger paints
- ⋅⋅ smoke signals
- ⋅⋅ pendulum

Sky Watcher

We humans have always been entranced by the sky—and sky wonders—for as long as we have had records. Stone circles and burial chambers were aligned with solstices, while Chaco Canyon's famous Sun Dagger casts shadows that mark both solstices and equinoxes. The great pyramid at Chichén Itzá was aligned so that a slithering snake of light appeared on its steps during the equinoxes; a window at Machu Picchu's Temple of the Sun aligned with the summer solstice. We have always been sky watchers.

But it wasn't only the changing seasons that inspired our ancestors to align their buildings or carve suns and moons into stone panels. The symbols of the animals they hunted and the gods who were worshipped are commonly found across cultures. If the Ancients couldn't write, at least they could communicate in a language of symbols. And boy, could they build.

And, see omens. Stories associated with comets are found in many cultures, usually accompanied by a sense of foreboding. The Romans saw a comet after the assassination of Julius Caesar, with some saying it meant he had become a god. In England, Halley's Comet was blamed for causing the Black Death. Of course, it seems that Halley popping up in 1066 turned out pretty well for William the Conqueror.

I have spent decades collecting the images of pictographs and petroglyphs throughout the American Southwest. As I noted in my previous book *Ancestral Tarot,* just standing on a cliff face and touching something you know was inscribed hundreds of years ago takes you tumbling back through time. I know that the record keeper of the tribe stood in this very spot while using rocks to chisel away the desert varnish. There, he told the story of life, capturing not only the movement of sun and moon, but also that of an exploding star—a supernova—of 1054.

This month let's call on an ancestor who brought the heavens to Earth by building an astronomical site or who captured celestial events in stone or paint. Your ancestor—in this life or another—could have chipped a lunar eclipse into a wall at Canyon de Chelly (de-shay) or helped configure the Parque Arqueológico do Solstício in Brazil.

To make the connection, you'll draw card position 1 in this spread from the Courts and position 2 from the Majors. Randomly draw the remaining positions from the entire deck.

1. My ancestor (Court card)

2. My ancestor's world (Major Arcana)

3. The ancestor's karmic influence on me

4. The ancestor's karmic influence on me that needs healing

5. My intergenerational sky magic inheritance

6. How can I best connect with this ancestor?

7. What solar or lunar symbols can I create to honor this ancestor?

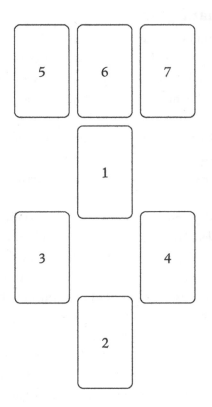

Before digging into each card's meaning, use your supplementary cards and pendulum to accurately place this ancestor in a time and a locale.

My ancestor was the Page of Swords, a young male who lived in 17th-century Egypt. During his short life he tried to learn how to calculate the motions of the planets and stars. His was a fast-moving world in which I believe he worked as an apprentice without much autonomy.

Who did you draw and what was their message for you? Does their life karmically impact your own in a surprising way? What magic did you inherit from the sky watcher? Not surprisingly for me it was a love of the sky and the stars.

Solar or Lunar Symbols

The seventh position in the spread you just did was fascinating for me. I hope it was for you as well. My card was the Three of Swords. How could I create a lunar or solar symbol using this card as a way of celebrating my ancestor? For me, this meant creating a symbol much like what I saw on those rock walls.

This meant I couldn't get very fancy because if you've ever tried to chip a design into a stone, you'll know it's hard. For the Three of Swords, I decided to simply use three lines to honor my ancestor: one for his life, one for his path, and one for his connection to me.

How do you do more advanced work, especially if—like me—you have no artistic talent? Begin with a basic shape like the three lines and add a symbol that's meaningful for you and your ancestor. I'm not 100 percent sure, but I might try to morph those three lines into three runic glyphs. But they need to make sense as the spread position was about honoring this ancestor. What have you decided to create?

As diviners, we work with symbols all the time. Do you keep a Symbol Log? That's a section in your grimoire where you draw a symbol and then add your interpretation. This works well when creating glyphs of your own, sigils, or when assigning meaning to your casting charms.

If you've created your symbol as you've determined it from card 7, what next? To honor this ancestor, what will you do? Some options would be:

- burning the paper
- drawing the symbol on a wood disk
- burying it
- placing it under starlight
- energizing it with a favorite crystal

The possibilities are many; however, I suggest ritualizing your symbol work using the energy you feel from this ancestor.

By the way, can I say that my ancestor's karmic influence on me was the exact same card I drew in August for the karma to be banished? No coincidence.

Equal Day and Night

Since this is the month of the fall equinox, when day and night are equal, I want you to ask your sky magician to help with whatever issues you might have staying balanced. For many of us, finding an equilibrium in work and play is probably our most difficult challenge. Or maybe that's just me. As you do this spread, I'd like to add one more component: crystals.

First, shuffle the entire tarot or oracle deck, then draw four cards. For the third card, draw down in the deck until you get to a Court card.

1. My balance at this time of this equinox

2. Where I can improve balance?

3. Is there an ancestor who can help me? (Draw a Court card.)

4. Shadow self (optional): What am I not taking responsibility for?

Once you've drawn all four cards, use your polished stones or crystals and place one on each card. The stones you choose are up to you. Does the stone or crystal make a difference in how you interpret the card? My balance card was the Nine of Pentacles, which I associate with leisure after rewarding work. The crystal, which I drew randomly, was a lapis lazuli. I was surprised that the calm of the blue stone actually changed how I felt about the card—it made it feel magical. As I write this, I realize that the stone you pick can be used energetically to change this spread and your balance.

Here's what I mean. The spread has four positions. Use those four as the basis for an arrangement of stones in a crystal grid. Build your grid with the intention of improving your equinox balance. Once your first four stones are placed, add other stones to create the balance you feel you need. I've recommended two books on crystal grids in Appendix A.

Messages in Paint and Fire

Since you're working with an ancestor who could find magic in equinoxes and solstices, you know they could also communicate via symbols. In other words, they could align themselves with sky beings and use that energy to work their magic on Earth.

This month you're going to do the same, except instead of interpreting clouds or waves or bird flights you're going to cocreate, with your ancestor, a message that's personal to you and you alone.

Here's what you'll need:

Method 1: A few finger paints. A basic set of red, blue, and yellow works. Or, if your kids use finger paints, you already have what you need.

Method 2: Candle smoke

Both methods: Paper heavy enough to get wet or go through smoke

Finger Paints

Start with a question that relates to your sky-based ancestor. Then, put whatever finger paint colors on the paper you're guided to include. Now comes the hard part for my Virgo-self: stick your hands into the paint. Then, just follow the energy. This isn't a head thing; this is an intuitive thing. You'll intuitively know which direction to move your fingers and you'll know when to stop. Don't try to paint anything—let your hands lead the way. Then stop.

Keeping your question in mind, look for answers in the paint. Be sure to turn the paper in all directions. You will be surprised at what appears.

I asked for knowledge about a deck I want to create. In my finger paints I saw several fish, two bird heads, twisted tree trunks, a fairy face, and feathers.

If you're having problems seeing anything, ask your ancestor for guidance. Pull out your cards, runes, pendulum, and other divination tools if you need clarifiers.

Smoke Signals

If you don't want to try finger paints, you can also ask your ancestor to help you via smoke signals.

Start with a question, ask the ancestor for help, then light a candle with intent. Take a small square of paper (perhaps 4 x 5 inches) and slowly move in through the candle flame. Don't go so slow that your paper catches on fire.

Stop when you feel it's time to stop. Then, turn the paper over and look at the smoke marks. What do you see? How does this answer your question?

You probably don't need for me to say this, but be sure to add this to your grimoire.

Finding Balance

If you still need help with your question or with finding balance, get out your pendulum and a plain piece of paper.

On the paper write the areas of your life that you want to check for being under- or overenergized. This is a sample but be sure to put down your own areas of concern.

Family   Work

Play

Spirituality   Relationships

Next, ask where you need balance. Then, hold your pendulum over each word. You'll get a quick answer. Next, ask where you have invested too much energy, and repeat the process holding your pendulum over each word. By the time you finish, you'll know where to redistribute your energy.

One last thing to check out: does your state of internal balance correlate in any way with the movement of the sun through either solstices, equinoxes, or daily motion?

Daily Draw

I hope you were able to locate this ancestor in time and space using your supplementary cards and pendulum. Did you find someone who helped build a solar or lunar observatory or sacred site?

As you draw your morning or evening cards for September, how can you relate them to your own sky magic? Are your cards about building (Pentacles), planning (Swords), blessing (Cups), or initiation (Wands)?

If you draw a predominance of Major Arcana, what does this tell you about your connection with this ancestor? Are they asking you to make your own magical site (Magician) or perhaps encouraging you to dig into solar or lunar magic far below the surface (Moon)?

OCTOBER

Elemental Magic: Omen Magic

October Tools

- ⟡ tarot
- ⟡ sidewalk oracles
- ⟡ the clairs
- ⟡ charms or stones

Sign Reader

So much of ancestral work—or any kind of divination for that matter—is about recognizing and interpreting signs. I'm telling you, it's impossible to go through your day without seeing dozens of them, both in nature and human-made.

The ancestors send us messages all the time via signs. Sometimes we're conscious enough to receive them, but other times we tune them out. Stress, lack of sleep, busyness, mind-altering substances—they all gum up the works, making it much harder to get a message. But if you're a clean receiver . . . Wow!

Here's one example I'm sure you can relate to: I was mulling over a relationship, torn between staying or leaving. In the exact moments I was considering what was best for me, Carole King came on Pandora, singing about why "It's Too Late."

Could the message be any clearer?

Here's one more. I was driving, wondering if it would be a good thing for me to buy a new telescope and return to my lifelong love of astronomy. I looked up and, in the clouds, I clearly saw a goddess following an eagle. I immediately thought of the Andromeda Galaxy and the constellation Aquila, the eagle. That was a definite yes.

Signs can appear in a variety of ways, and I'll try and put them into categories to help you get an idea of their range. Please note that this is *not* a comprehensive list.

Natural World

- leaves
- shadows
- clouds
- sticks (often you can see rune symbols in sticks)
- water
- stones
- rain
- wind

Animals

- cats
- birds
- fish
- insects
- foxes
- coyotes
- dogs

Human-Made

- business signs
- street signs
- billboards
- walls

- ⟡ fences
- ⟡ box labels

- ⟡ music

Plants

- ⟡ weeds
- ⟡ flowers
- ⟡ trees

- ⟡ moss
- ⟡ lawns

For October—the second month of fall—your ancestor is going to help you add reading signs to your many magical skills. You may not think this is as cool or as powerful as writing spells or engaging in weather magic, but being able to spot and interpret signs can be one of your most valuable skills because you don't need any tools beyond your own senses.

On one of my sidewalk oracle strolls I took a photo of a door. That door's energy bothered me so much I wouldn't walk down that street anymore. I posted the photo on Instagram, and an IG friend told me that when her little girl saw the picture, she said there was something bad behind the door. That door was the sign, and what was behind it was the message: there's nothing good here.

So, before you draw cards for your ancestor, take a moment and envision what it might feel like if you could read signs. What if this were your own, most potent magical skill? In what ways do you think you could use it?

Now let's connect with your omen diviner. Find your ancestor by drawing from the Court cards or visiting the Land of Tarot (Chapter 4). If you've tried only one of these methods so far in this book, please try the other.

I went to the Land of Tarot for this exercise, and this is what I found. There, I met the King of Swords. On an *RWS* card, he sits upright, facing forward. There's no side-eye here. On his throne are butterflies and behind him are clouds and birds. In some decks this King's robes are embellished with clouds and birds. He's intelligent and decisive, and rules by order and logic—all qualities of Air.

It's interesting that, in this version, the outside of the cloak is dreary gray while the inside is bright orange. Is this telling you that—a bit like a magician—what you see isn't always what you get? I drew a clarifier from my own oracle and got a card of clouds and birds as well! That confirms this King was the one who wanted to come forward.

Once you have your ancestor clearly in mind, ask about *their specific brand of magic*. Could they see weather signs or those of health, love, danger, or the water? Draw from the entire deck for this one.

I drew the Chariot. Again, this is one of those times when the deck you choose *really does matter*.

The *RWS* Chariot depicts the charioteer driving two sphinxes and wearing a star as a crown. *The Relative Tarot* shows a woman with a star crown and a background of stars. As it turns out, my King of Swords ancestor worked with star magic. I've known for a long time that this is my most powerful form of magic—so the Chariot confirmed it.

Who did you draw? And what was the magic?

By the way, I didn't keep drawing until I got a Major Arcana; it was just the first card off the top of the deck. What if I had drawn the Five of Cups? What form of magic do you think this would be?

Remember, when doing ancestral work, it's okay to go with first impressions. For example, with the Five of Cups, notice the imagery of the water in the river and the wine. If this were the card I drew, I'd say that my ancestor's way of receiving messages was by water gazing or water scrying. Think of Harry Potter sticking his head in the Pensieve.

But whatever you learned about your ancestor, let's be curious about how you could put the same skill into practice.

Do this next. Put all the cards back into the deck and reshuffle. Ask for the easiest way for you to read signs and ask how you can use signs for evidential divination—a type of divining that can be proven. Draw at least two cards, or more if you please.

Interpreting Signs—Practice Your Skills

Let's practice. Starting with a question or something that's been on your mind, take a walk, even if it's just in your neighborhood, or look out a window if that is easier.

At some point something is going to catch your eye.

I've already mentioned clouds, but that is just one possibility. Here are a few other examples of what signs might mean—keeping in mind that when I see a crow feather, it may mean something far different than if you see one.

> **Stones:** These can represent strength, being grounded, or being stuck. You'll get the stuck part if you've ever tried to dig up a rock that's huge or one that's cemented into an upscale parkway with a bunch of other rocks. (They hate that.)

> **Cats:** I see a lot of cats when I walk, and their energy can vary from "I'm invisible" to "What are you doing here?" to "You look kind of interesting." I really do try to let the cat do the talking.

Text: On one of my walks, I saw an empty beer box on top of a trash can and the name "rebel" popped out at me. I knew it was a message about being willing to do work that's outside the norm. Why? Because that's what I was thinking about during the walk.

Flowers: First, please know that flowers love being admired. And, even if you see a dozen of the same flower, they each have a different message. Look closely at any one of them that calls to you. If it's a daisy, does your mind immediately go to the childhood practice of "he loves me, he loves me not"? If this sounds familiar, did you notice that the flower didn't speak to you as much as your actions were a reaction to the flowers?

This is a practice I encourage you to do daily. I promise, you'll get to be an accurate diviner if you keep at it.

Signs of the Unseen

Just as someone living in Scotland can't see the constellation Carina (since it's visible only from the tropics southward), most of us can't see Spirit. This isn't to say it's impossible, but that it's not easy.

I've been following a spiritual path for decades and have thought a lot about why someone can see Spirit, feel Spirit, or hear messages. Which takes me to the *clairs*.

I can see spirit cats, and occasionally—especially when I'm super-focused on my tarot or ancestral work—I can see spirits. And, if I ask a question, I can hear an answer inside my head. If I'm truly distressed, I can hear an ancestor speaking somewhere in the room.

In *Ancestral Tarot* I gave examples of the ways you can experience Spirit, but here I want to talk about the clairs as the gateways that can help you receive signs that are unseen.

Clairaudience: The skill of clear hearing. You may hear voices, sounds, music in your head—or potentially audibly. In my case, the audible sound came when I was highly focused on my mom. I was having a bad day and I think my cry flew out into the world of Spirit and was heard. If you want to channel, clairaudience is a key component.

Clairsentience: The skill of clear feeling. You could call this your gut feeling. You can physically sense the emotions of others on the earth plane or in Spirit. Think about when you get goose bumps—it's usually when you feel something that you know is true. This is a great skill for an energy healer. But make sure you have good boundaries, or else you can drown in other people's feelings.

Clairvoyance: The skill of clear seeing. If you can see things from the past or the future flashing through your mind, you probably are clairvoyant. This is a skill for those of us who relate more to images than words. Clairvoyants typically see something that's going to happen before it happens. However, they can also use clairvoyance as a form of evidentiary mediumship. One of my clairvoyant friends can describe a place she's never seen. There's unmistakable evidence she is clairvoyant.

Clairalience: The skill of clear smelling. This is the ability to smell odors that don't exist on the physical plane. I've written before about my mother's ability to smell her mother's perfume and her brother's aftershave. It's a wonderful skill to have when working with an ancestor that you knew in life.

Claircognizance: The skill of clear knowing. For me this is a knowingness about something you have no knowledge of. I believe, when you're skilled at this, you're tapping into another lifetime or ancestral memories. You've heard me talk about Jessica Macbeth of *The Faeries' Oracle.* I can ask her about the most obscure topic, and she can tell me about it—even though there's no earthly reason she should have that knowledge.

Clairgustance: The skill of clear tasting. It's most often written about in terms of tapping into an ancestor with whom you share an important memory built around food. That could be your granny's spaghetti sauce or your aunt's green salsa. This is the clair about which I'm most uninformed, probably because I've never met anyone who has this skill.

If you want to work more with the Unseen—the clairs—begin by embracing silence. If you sit still for even a few minutes, you'll notice sounds or feelings that you didn't in your normal state of being. What catches your attention as you move through your room energetically? What stands out? Do you see, sense, feel, or otherwise experience something beyond your usual frame of reference?

Start with this easy practice and you'll soon discover which of the clairs is the best fit for how you receive. Or you may have more than one of the clairs. I'm best at clairaudience, but I have experienced both clairvoyance and clairsentience.

If you want to use one of these skills as a diviner, work in your grimoire by making daily predictions. Then give yourself ten to fifteen minutes every day to sit quietly and see what appears. Write it down and then check back. Sometimes what you experienced may not be proven for days or even weeks.

I have a kind of weird request: Before you leave October, look around you and see the many things in your house or apartment that symbolize *something*. Right now, I'm looking at a screaming goat that Fred gave me. I let it scream when I'm frustrated. My horse and buffalo Zuni fetishes bring me back to my roots as a history geek. The water bottle is my ticket to better health.

If you want a valuable exercise for improving your interpretative skills, start a Symbol Log in your grimoire. There won't be a test—but keeping a log and *practicing* will enhance your sign reading skills.

Daily Draw

If you want to draw tarot every day of October, great. But for a month of omen magic, try your crystals or polished stones or runes or charms and make a daily prediction with them instead. For example, if I drew a guitar charm, my prediction would be that at some point during my day a guitar would be significant. Maybe one of my neighbors would be playing or maybe some guy on a street corner.

Spend all month making daily predictions. I predict that on October 31 (Happy Halloween!) your predictive skills will be way better than they were on October 1.

NOVEMBER

Family Magic: Ancestral Magic

November Tools

- ⟡ tarot
- ⟡ altar

Guide to the Afterworld

November is a special month. You've heard that the veil between the living and the dead is thinnest at this time. That could be, but I think there's a simpler explanation. In early November, the globe is crisscrossed with the energy of millions honoring their dead. How could those on the other side of the veil ignore all the prayers going heavenward on All Souls' Day, All Saints' Day, Day of the Dead, Samhain, and the British Commonwealth's Remembrance Day?

So now, in your own form of remembrance, call in your ancestor who can serve as a guide to the afterworld—one who can show you how to peek through the veil and touch hearts with those whose hearts touch yours.

It's possible this ancestor, while incarnate, worked with the dying, comforted the grieving, or knew, in her own magical way, how to guide a lost soul across the River Styx. Meeting her will open a pathway that sparks with so much magic you might have a hard time keeping your eyes on your footing.

How to Begin

First, set your intention. Remember to do your pre-journey work of protecting yourself from any entity with a lower vibration or who does not have your best interest at heart.

The intention I set for myself was to meet an ancestor who could inject my ancestral work with a large dose of evidence-based information. What intention are you setting for yourself?

Once you've written your intention in your grimoire, shuffle the entire deck and draw down until you reach the first Court card.

I drew the King of Swords. What card did you draw?

I've always struggled a little with the Kings because they seem so detached. And—you must admit—is anyone more detached than *this* King? But when I thought about his qualities, I realized he would have been what we call an evidentiary clairvoyant—one whose visions could be proven. This is exactly what I'm looking for.

Once you've found your ancestor, use your supplementary cards to find the time in which they lived, as well as their gender. If you want to use your pendulum to find where they lived, that's even better.

For your Ancestral Grimoire: What do you think about adding a small map of the area in which this ancestor lived?

Next, draw down in the deck until you reach a Major Arcana. For this month, this is the card that represents *the way this ancestor can help with your intent*. If you get a "scary" card, don't worry. Look for the message beyond the obvious. For example, I got the Tower (Major Arcana 16), which tells me that working with this ancestor is going to shake up the foundation of some of my beliefs—especially the ones that need a good shake.

Finally, draw any number of cards from the entire deck to clarify the message as well as your needed action. If you want to use an oracle or Lenormand deck or runes too, it's all good.

If you're having problems getting to know who the ancestor is or what their magical power was, visit the Land of Tarot and have a conversation. I guarantee the ancestor will love giving you the scoop.

I wanted to know exactly what my King of Swords could help me with in practical terms. For example, I drew the Six of Swords, so I know I was being told that I wasn't allowing a space for evidentiary clairvoyance to blossom. *I'm not out of choppy waters yet.*

Because there are two people in the boat plus the boatman, I think I'll be working with someone more skilled in this than I am. There's more to be revealed here.

I also drew the Ten of Pentacles—the legacy card. Based on my intuition—and you're using yours too, right?—I knew that this skill is a family legacy. In other words: Ask the ancestors.

Lastly, I got a message from the Five of Pentacles: Make my space sacred or go someplace sacred. Evidential clairvoyance will be easier for me there. As soon as I saw the card, I knew that I was going to go sit quietly in the chapel at the Mission San Diego de Alcalá as it's my favorite sacred space.

When you've finished journaling your ancestral adventure, jump on board my time machine. Let's go back to ancient Egypt as it's a culture with strong ties to the afterlife and the rebirth of souls.

Ma'at—A Spread of Balance

Just as the Egyptians sought balance—called Ma'at, for the goddess of justice and balance—so do most of us. I saw a meme on Instagram not long ago addressing what we *think* is balance (money-work balance) versus what *is* balance: work, play, health, friends, nutrition, emotions, relationships. Borrowing a page from Egyptian life, let's compare your balance with that of your November ancestor.

To do this, choose all the areas of life where you want to add to your wholeness. Don't just use mine—pick the important areas of your own life. Next, select a Court card—upright, and you can choose by looking—that represents you today and one for your ancestor's life. Then, draw a card in each area for both you and for the ancestor. Once all your cards are drawn, it's easy to see the area where the ancestor can best help with balance.

I chose the Knight of Pentacles for myself, and if you remember, my ancestor was the King of Swords.

AREA OF LIFE	KING OF SWORDS	KNIGHT OF PENTACLES
Play/relax	The Fool (0)	The World (21)
Friends	The Sun (19)	The Star (17)
Work	Eight of Wands	Six of Pentacles (rx)
Health	Nine of Swords (rx)	Nine of Cups
Emotions	Nine of Pentacles	Six of Cups (rx)

Although this draw was about finding balance, it can also tell you worlds about your ancestor's own life. Ma'at—let's aim for it. While we both are balanced when it comes to friends, my ancestor was far more balanced in emotions and I think much more willing to jump off that cliff of play than I am.

Since you're working with your guide to the afterworld, will you allow me one more spread before leaving Egypt? This one's a bonus.

Let's Talk about Crocodiles

In ancient Egypt, the crocodile was the protector of the Nile, and some say the protector of Egypt herself. Brave was the invader who tried to cross the croc-riddled river. According to the science guys, these prehistoric-looking critters have been on the planet for more than eighty-five million years.

Sobek, the crocodile god, was the symbol of the pharaoh's power. Thousands of croc mummies have been found in Egypt, sacrificed to Sobek to keep the river safe. This reverence—and fear—was probably born from self-preservation as even today crocs are responsible for more deaths in the Nile than any other animal.

I know you've already found your November ancestor, but as a bonus, do you want to ask for a magical ancestor who was also a protector as you navigate the thin veil? If so, let's find your crocodile.

Protector of Your Nile

This time you're going to use an oracle deck. Because you're working with the protective nature of the crocodile, you may want to choose an animal or nature deck. There are only four positions in this spread, each relating to an anatomical part of the croc, plus one Court card for your protector.

1. My Nile (what needs protecting)—draw from a Major Arcana

2. The tail: The past

3. The eyes: The future

4. The jaw: The present

5. The Protector (Court card)

What did you learn? Who is your crocodile in the Ancestral Realm? And what is the message about protection? Who appeared and why?

Once you've completed this spread, we end our journey on the Nile.

Honoring Your Ancestors

One thing many cultures share in late October or early November is honoring those who came before us. Before leaving November, how can you honor your ancestors? After all, you are what your ancestors dreamed into being.

Whether you celebrate Samhain, Day of the Dead, or All Souls' and All Saints' Day, the ancestors are happy to be remembered.

1. In what way can I honor my ancestors?

2. What have they helped me learn this year?

3. How can I use their advice to help others?

Día de los Muertos (Day of the Dead)

Although I hate leaving Egypt, I couldn't bid farewell to November without mentioning the Day of the Dead, celebrated November 1–2. This celebration has its origins in Mexico going back to the time of the Aztecs. More than six centuries ago, the Aztecs kept skulls on altars to honor the dead—just as is practiced today with popular sugar skulls. When the Spanish conquered the Aztecs, their celebrations were incorporated into the Catholic All Saints' Day (November 1) and All Souls' Day (November 2).

By the way, the Aztecs believed that members of the royal family could conjure dead ancestors for advice or favors. And their soothsayers could interpret dreams and omens, sometimes casting maize kernels on the floor or into the water, seeking patterns that predicted future events.

There are numerous symbols associated with Day of the Dead, each with a specific meaning. This is the time the dead return to visit the living. Accompanying them is a dog who guides and protects the souls of the dead. By the way, the dog that accompanies the dead is a xoloitzcuintli, also known as a xolo. Marigolds are used to line the pathways as the bright color and strong scent help attract the dead.

Ofrendas (altars) are constructed to pay respects to the departed and hold not only candles, but also objects associated with the loved one. This can vary from a piece of clothing to cigarettes, a bottle of tequila, candy (like the candy bar I leave by my mom's photo), letters, or love notes. You'll also find a loaf of *pan de muerto* (bread of the dead).

One of the most recognizable symbols of this day is a sugar skull. If you've never seen sugar skulls, they're really something special—made of sugar and decorated with painted flowers, they sometimes bear the name of the departed across the forehead. Graves are cleaned and families often have a large meal in the cemetery.

Día de los Muertos is a time in Mexican culture to both remember and pay respects to those who are no longer living.

What will be placed on your *ofrenda* on these days? If you think about a special ancestor that you knew, what will honor them? A special food or drink? Flowers or a photo of themselves that would make them proud? If you follow Día de los Muertos tradition, your altar will include marigolds. But if your ancestor loved roses, let it be roses.

On this day—regardless of which path you follow—pour the ancestors a cup of coffee and leave a plate of food out for them as you eat. You will be blessed.

Daily Draw

November is the most magical ancestral month of all. As you draw cards each morning and each evening, interpret them relative to your family. Then, use them to discover new ways to honor their lives and their gift of life to you.

DECEMBER

Family Magic: Magical You

December Tools

- ✧ tarot
- ✧ personal card
- ✧ manifesting ball or ornament
- ✧ sigil

Setting Sail

This month, we set sail. Where our voyage will end, I cannot tell as the destination is yours to discover . . .

But I do know where to start, and that is standing on the undiscovered shore of December. This is a month of sparkly lights, Christmas trees, parties, and overindulgence. Even though our internal clocks tell us we should still be sleeping within our winter caves, celebrations lure us out of hibernation.

If September's equinox brought balance, December is a month of maintaining that balance. The year is almost gone, and if you're anything like me, you will have accomplished much, ignored much, gotten lazy about much, and discovered how much is too much. But you've also had twelve months to discover your lineage of ancestral magic. That's a perfect place to enter the first month of winter, where you can meet the real ghosts of past, present, and future—the ancestors.

December's Magician

Let's begin as we do each month by setting an intention to find an ancestor you can work with throughout this month. Perhaps you want to know more about your ancestor's magical abilities or how they can help you find yours. This is the month of magical You, so the decisions are all yours. Take it away.

The Ghosts of December Spread

Separate your tarot deck into Major Arcana, Minor Arcana, and Court cards. Draw position 1 from the Court cards, position 7 from the Major Arcana, and the rest from the Minors.

1. Who is the ghost (ancestor) of the present—the one closest to me today? (Court card)

2. What is their message about my past year?

3. What is their message for the coming year?

4. How can they help me end the year successfully?

5. What was their magic?

6. How can they help with my magic?

7. What was the theme of their life? (Major Arcana)

8. What is their gift to me?

9. What form of magic did I inherit from this ancestor?

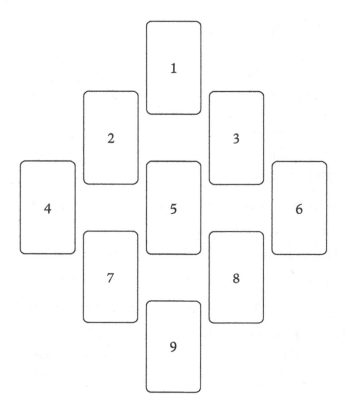

I'm not going to get into my own cards except to say that my December ancestor passed along her ability to walk the narrow line between this world and the next.

As you delve into this spread remember that every card in a tarot deck has both a message and a lesson. If you draw a Seven of Swords, for example, for position 4 in the Ghost of December spread, what's the message you're hearing and what's the lesson? Is it possible your ancestor is suggesting you're best served by leaving some things behind but taking other things (ideas) forward? Is the lesson about the risks associated with dishonesty? These nine cards, when added to your grimoire, can pull back the curtain on much that's been previously hidden.

December's Shadows

And speaking of the hidden, December can be a time of dark shadows. The joy felt by many can be a deep wound for someone with painful memories of Decembers past or present. And just because something unpleasant happened decades ago doesn't mean the wound is healed. Although it's counterintuitive, the energies of December support shadow work, perhaps more than any other month. If this resonates for you, please go ahead, and do this spread using tarot or an oracle.

1. What limiting belief about myself did I learn in childhood?

2. How does that belief manifest today?

3. How can I confront the belief in a healthy manner?

4. What action can I take to move beyond this belief?

5. What magic can my December ancestor work on my behalf?

These cards won't magically erase your triggers, but hopefully they will ease a little of the pain. My very first Christmas without my mom was the worst of my life. That pain remains, but my December ancestor assures me that love fills the future.

The You That Is Magic

If you began this book last January, you may remember creating a single card that represented you. I'd love it if you'd do another. This time craft a card that represents your own personal magic.

Materials needed:

A tarot card (optional)   Pictures of your choosing

An index card   Glue

If you know your own most potent magic, you won't need to draw a card. But if you don't, shuffle the entire deck, asking what you need to know about your own magic this month. Draw one card, then make your own version of that card. You may want to sketch the card in your grimoire or create one using a blank index card and copyright-free images found online or in magazines.

As I said in January, this isn't the same as creating a wish board. It's far more magical than that as it plants your magical flag on this day.

Although I know my own magic, I did go ahead and draw a card. Not surprisingly it was the Six of Cups—for me, the ancestor card. This is how that card reflects my magic today.

What does yours look like?

Manifesting Your Own Magic

What do you think about creating a manifestation object that relates directly to your December ancestor? You'll need a craft store plain glass ball or ornament. You know the kind I mean—they have a little metal cap that you can pull off, allowing you to place your magical goodies within the ball. What you choose to place inside the globe depends on what you're trying to manifest or the magical ancestor you're working with. It's a little like choosing the things you place in a rattle—think about the energy.

What type of magic do you want to manifest? If you know the answer to this question, you know what goes into your glass ball. I drew cards asking my ancestor for suggestions to craft a sphere that would give me the strength to enter the new year with optimism, a willingness to change, happiness with my family and friends, and courage to jump off yet another cliff. Among the objects were a photo, a sprig of rosemary, one of pine, a tiny piece of agapanthus (a flower), a dollhouse-size book, and a tiny craft store bird (a cardinal). I also added a holly berry. There's more, but you get the idea.

If you feel superclose to the December ancestor—or any of the others— confer with them about your intent and what should go into the glass ball. I'd suggest starting early in December as sometimes it can take a few weeks to carefully decide on your objects. If you remember, it took me two weeks to make a manifestation jar in February. Another way to think about this is that your December ancestor is in a great position to help you craft a sphere that can take you into the new year and the manifestation of your magical skills.

Let your intuition be your guide. If you need to draw cards or runes or visit the Land of Tarot, follow where your own energy leads you.

Deep in Winter Ancestral Tarot Spread

December is supposed to be a magical time, but sometimes we get so hung up on what should be that we forget the magic that we can create on our own. This can be simple acts of charity, a prayer of gratitude, a healing sent to a distant friend, or even a beautifully dressed candle.

If you need a reminder of all that magic, this spread will help reignite it. Use either a tarot or oracle deck.

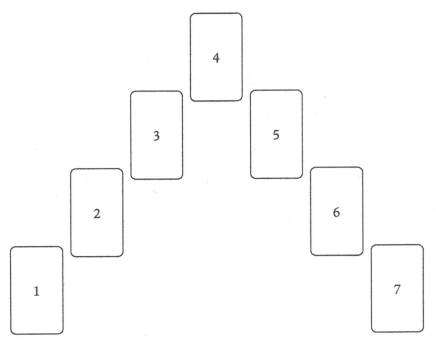

1. What magical belief needs healing?

2. What magical belief needs creating?

3. What needs my fire?

4. What magical ability is waiting to be seen?

5. What is my unique magic?

6. What dream can come true?

7. What needs to stay frozen until spring?

What Have You Discovered?

I don't know about you, but I've learned a lot about my own magical skills this year. My revelations have to do with working with ancestors who could merge their magic with star magic. As the year ends, let's both create a sigil for our magical lineage and our own magic.

If you've forgotten how to create a sigil, refer back to Chapter 5. Each of the sigils you've created this year carries its own magic. But the December one is the most powerful as it's an ancestral magical symbol that will be part of your life from now on.

And in case you're wondering, the one I'm showing you here is not the one I created for myself. That one is private—as yours should be as well.

You can either create a sigil of symbols or use the alpha-grid method associating a letter with a number.

As a reminder, these are the numerology equivalents to letters:

1	2	3	4	5	6	7	8	9
a, j, s	b, k, t	c, l, u	d, m, v	e, n, w	f, o, x	g, p, y	h, q, z	i, r

And the nine-panel grid for sketching your sigil looks like this:

1	2	3
4	5	6
7	8	9

You're going to choose a single word or two that represent what your ancestral magical lineage is for you. Next, you'll sketch it in your grid, after eliminating any repeating numbers. Here's a simple sample. The words "old faith" translate to: 6-3-4-6-1-9-2-8. Eliminating repeating numbers, I'm left with 6-3-4-1-9-2-8:

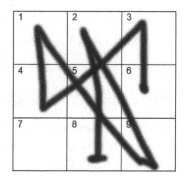

Is it just me, or does this sigil look a little like a lopsided star?

What you do with this sigil is a personal decision. Will you bury it, hide it, tattoo it, carve it into an apple to be eaten, or something else? This sigil and you are meant to be lifelong companions.

Daily Draw

Because December is a time of gift-giving, I suggest for your daily draws to interpret each card as a gift. Regardless of how "negative" the card appears, how can you receive it as a true blessing in your life?

A December Gift

Because they love you, the ancestors want to leave you with something precious—a magical gift made only for you. Like your sigil, it's something you can carry for a lifetime.

Draw three cards:

1. The gift

2. Its magical element

3. Its power

TURNING THE TABLES

You've had twelve months to ask questions of your ancestors. Now it's the ancestors' turn to ask you. Draw one card randomly for each ancestor's question, or draw from Major Arcana, Minor Arcana, or Court cards. It's your choice.

January

The ancestor of inherited magic wants to know:
What part of your inherited magic needs more scrutiny?

February

Your ancestor of manifestation is curious:
What can you manifest that helps others?

March

Your ancestor of healing wonders:
What healing modality is the best fit for you?

April

Your ancestor of land magic asks:
How are you acknowledging the guardians of the land?

May

Your moon magician shines the light on:
Which of your magical tools needs to be dialed up?

June

Your solstice magician waves his wand to ask:
How can you heal from the negative words of other people?

July

Your weather magician is curious to know:
How can you express your truth?

August

Your ancestor of past lives would like to know:
How can you use a past life as an inspiration now?

September

Your sky magician asks you to look to the stars and answer:
How can you manifest positive change in the world?

October

Your omen magician wonders if you're listening to the signs:
What messages do the birds have for you today?

November

Your guide to the afterlife asks:
How are you helping heal negative family patterns?

December

Your magical self asks:
How can you claim your power?

BEFORE YOU GO

At the beginning of the book, I asked you to do two things. Now, I'm doing the same.

Answer this question:

Today, I know my most potent form of magic is

_____.

Next, draw a single card to answer the question:

Why was I really here?

CLOSING THOUGHTS

Although I'm not in the room with you, I do metaphorically sit with you and the ancestors. I know that time is always a factor. You may work with only a month or two's worth of magic, or you may spend a year doing every single spread and project. How short or how long it takes doesn't make that much difference. It's how you see yourself as the most recent member of your magical lineage that does.

You're the product of thousands of years of evolutionary changes, cultural divides, wars, celebrations, pandemics, and the best and worst of humankind. Along the way you managed to be born into a family line with the power to change at least part of the world.

Magic—at its core—is the investment of intent and energy into creation. What will be yours?

APPENDIX A

RESOURCES

Books

Ancestral Tarot: Uncover Your Past and Chart Your Future by Nancy Hendrickson (Weiser Books, 2021).

Archetypal Tarot: What Your Birth Card Reveals about Your Personality, Path, and Potential by Mary K. Greer (Weiser Books, 2021).

The Art of Celtic Seership: How to Divine from Nature and the Otherworld by Caitlin Matthews (Watkins Publishing, 2021).

The Book of Candle Magic: Candle Spell Secrets to Change Your Life by Madame Pamita (Llewellyn Publications, 2020).

Brigid's Light: Tending the Ancestral Flame of the Beloved Celtic Goddess by Cairelle Crow and Laura Louella (Weiser Books, 2022).

Crystal Gridwork: The Power of Crystals and Sacred Geometry to Heal, Protect and Inspire by Kiera Fogg (Weiser Books, 2018)

Daily Magic: Spells and Rituals for Making the Whole Year Magical by Judika Illes (HarperOne, 2021).

Encyclopedia of 5,000 Spells: The Ultimate Reference Book for the Magical Arts by Judika Illes (HarperOne, 2009).

The Faeries' Oracle by Jessica Macbeth and Brian Froud (Fireside, 2000).

Holistic Tarot: An Integrative Approach to Using Tarot for Personal Growth by Benebell Wen (North Atlantic Books, 2015).

An Introduction to Crystal Grids: Daily Rituals for Your Heart, Health, and Happiness by Karen Frazier (Rockridge Press, 2020).

Kitchen Table Tarot by Melissa Cynova (Llewellyn Publications, 2017).

Lunar Alchemy: Everyday Moon Magic to Transform Your Life by Shaheen Miro (Weiser Books, 2020).

Mary K. Greer's 21 Ways to Read a Tarot Card by Mary K. Greer (Llewellyn Publications, 2011).

Moon Spells: How to Use the Phases of the Moon to Get What You Want by Diane Ahlquist (Adams Media, 2002).

Seventy-Eight Degrees of Wisdom: A Tarot Journey to Self-Awareness by Rachel Pollack (Weiser Books, 2019).

Tarot for Troubled Times by Theresa Reed and Shaheen Miro (Weiser Books, 2019).

The Tarot Handbook: Practical Applications of Ancient Visual Symbols by Angeles Arrien (Jeremy P. Tarcher/Putnam, 1997).

Tarot Inspired Life: Use the Cards to Enhance Your Life by Jaymi Elford (Llewellyn Publications, 2019).

Tarot: No Questions Asked: Mastering the Art of Intuitive Reading by Theresa Reed (Weiser Books, 2020).

Decks

Blooming Cat Tarot by Jen Brown

Bonestone & Earthflesh Tarot by Avalon Cameron

Dark Goddess Tarot by Ellen Lorenzi-Prince

Dust II Onyx Tarot by Courtney Alexander

The Green Witch Oracle by Cheralyn Darcey

The Healing Power of Witchcraft by Meg Rosenbriar

The Hoodoo Tarot by Tayannah Lee McQuillar, artwork by Katelan V. Foisy

The Literary Witches Oracle by Taisia Kitaiskaia and Katy Horan

The Lunar Nomad Oracle by Shaheen Miro

Modern Witch Tarot by Lisa Sterle

Moonology Oracle by Yasmin Boland

Queen of the Moon Oracle by Stacey Demarco

The Relative Tarot: Your Ancestral Blueprint for Self-Discovery by Carrie Paris

The Robin Wood Tarot by Robin Wood

Spirit Oracle by Carrie Paris

Apps

Tarot

If I love a deck, I'll often purchase it as an app as well as a physical deck. With an app I can enlarge the images for a better look at the symbols. The Fool's Dog has a free Tarot Sampler with sixty different decks; it's a great choice if you're unsure of the type of deck you want to use.

Astrology

Astro Gold

Astrology Zone

Planetary Hours

The Sky

The Moon (iOS, Android)

Moon Phases (iOS, Android)

My Moon Phase (iOS, Android)

Night Sky (iOS)

Sky Map (Android)

SkyView (iOS, Android)

Stellarium (Desktop version is free, iOS app has a fee)

Websites

Build Your Own Bindrune *www.nordicrunes.info/runebuilder.php*

Labyrinth Locator *labyrinthlocator.com*

Nancy's Patreon *patreon.com/sageandshadow*

Salem Witch Trials *salem.lib.virginia.edu*

Survey of Scottish Witchcraft *www.shca.ed.ac.uk*

UK Tarot Conference *tarotconference.co.uk*

Vintage Cookbooks *gutenberg.org*

What Phase of the Moon Were You Born? *MoonGiant.com*

Witch with Me Community *witchwithme.com*

Podcasts

The Archetypal Tarot Podcast, Julienne Givot and Cyndera Quakenbush

Between the Worlds, Amanda Yates Garcia

The Fat Feminist Witch, Paige Vanderbeck

Tarot Bytes, Theresa Reed

Tarot for the Wild Soul, Lindsay Mack

Tarot Visions, Rose Red

Wildly Tarot Podcast, Holly and Esther

APPENDIX B

THE CHARTS

Minor Arcana Made Easy

	WANDS	CUPS	SWORDS	PENTACLES
Ace	Inspiration	Joy	New project	Abundance
Two	Waiting	Partnership	Decisions	Multitasking
Three	Optimism	Celebration	Old hurts	Cooperation
Four	Harmony	Boredom	Rest	Greedy
Five	Challenges	Regret	Conflict	Needy
Six	Victory	Nostalgia	Escape	Philanthropist
Seven	Resolve	Confusion	Stealth	Slow growth

Minor Arcana Made Easy (*continued*)

	WANDS	CUPS	SWORDS	PENTACLES
Eight	Speed	Discontent	Trapped	Craftsmanship
Nine	Protection	Wish granted	Worry	Solitude
Ten	Burdens	Bliss	Defeat	Security
Page	Free spirit	Seeker	Messenger	Deliberate
Knight	Courageous	Romantic	Idea-seeker	Practical
Queen	Dramatic	Sensitive	Honest	Resourceful
King	Adventure	Empathetic	Decisive	Generous

Major Arcana Correspondences

MAJOR ARCANA	ELEMENT	ASTROLOGICAL SIGN
Fool	Air	Uranus
Magician	Air	Mercury
High Priestess	Water	Moon
Empress	Earth	Venus
Emperor	Fire	Aries
Hierophant	Earth	Taurus
Lovers	Air	Gemini
Chariot	Water	Cancer
Strength	Fire	Leo

MAJOR ARCANA	ELEMENT	ASTROLOGICAL SIGN
Hermit	Earth	Virgo
Wheel of Fortune	Fire	Jupiter
Justice	Air	Libra
Hanged Man	Water	Neptune
Death	Water	Scorpio
Temperance	Fire	Sagittarius
Devil	Earth	Capricorn
Tower	Fire	Mars
Star	Air	Aquarius
Moon	Water	Pisces
Sun	Fire	Sun
Judgement	Fire	Pluto
World	Earth	Saturn

Major Arcana

	Tarot	Sign/Planet	Element	Keywords
0	Fool	Uranus	Air	Innocence, trust
1	Magician	Mercury	Air	Manifestation
2	High Priestess	Moon	Water	Inner knowing
3	Empress	Venus	Earth	Creativity
4	Emperor	Aries	Fire	Foundations
5	Hierophant	Taurus	Earth	Teachings
6	Lovers	Gemini	Air	Relationships
7	Chariot	Cancer	Water	Movement
8	Strength	Leo	Fire	Mind over matter
9	Hermit	Virgo	Earth	Reflection
10	Wheel of Fortune	Jupiter	Fire	Chance
11	Justice	Libra	Air	Balance
12	Hanged Man	Neptune	Water	Stillness
13	Death	Scorpio	Water	Change
14	Temperance	Sagittarius	Fire	Blending
15	Devil	Capricorn	Earth	Addiction
16	Tower	Mars	Fire	Destruction
17	Star	Aquarius	Air	Hope
18	Moon	Pisces	Water	Hidden
19	Sun	Sun	Fire	Brilliant
20	Judgement	Pluto	Fire	New life
21	The World	Saturn	Earth	Completion

Lenormand Keywords

1	Rider	Message
2	Clover	Little luck
3	Ship	Voyage
4	House	Home
5	Tree	Slow growth/health
6	Clouds	Confusion
7	Snake	Deception
8	Coffin	Ending
9	Bouquet	Invitation
10	Scythe	Cutting
11	Whip	Repetition
12	Birds	Chatter
13	Child	New beginning
14	Fox	Trickery
15	Bear	Leader
16	Stars	Inspiration
17	Stork	Change
18	Dog	Loyalty
19	Tower	Authority
20	Garden	Social gathering
21	Mountain	Challenge
22	Crossroads	Decision
23	Mice	Decrease
24	Heart	Love
25	Ring	Commitment
26	Book	Knowledge
27	Letter	Communication
28	Man	Male
29	Woman	Female
30	Lily	Wisdom

31	Sun	Success
32	Moon	Emotion
33	Key	Solution
34	Fish	Abundance
35	Anchor	Stability
36	Cross	Burden

Runes

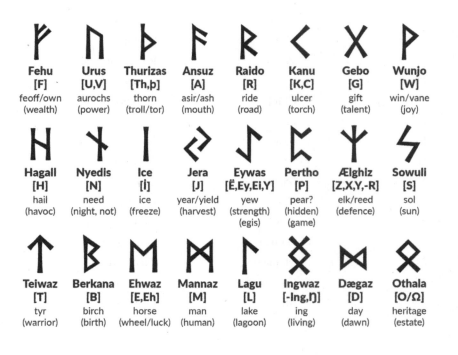

Fehu	Urus	Thurizas	Ansuz	Raido	Kanu	Gebo	Wunjo
[F]	[U,V]	[Th,þ]	[A]	[R]	[K,C]	[G]	[W]
feoff/own	aurochs	thorn	asir/ash	ride	ulcer	gift	win/vane
(wealth)	(power)	(troll/tor)	(mouth)	(road)	(torch)	(talent)	(joy)

Hagall	Nyedis	Ice	Jera	Eywas	Pertho	Ælghiz	Sowuli
[H]	[N]	[I]	[J]	[Ë,Ey,Ei,Y]	[P]	[Z,X,Y,-R]	[S]
hail	need	ice	year/yield	yew	pear?	elk/reed	sol
(havoc)	(night, not)	(freeze)	(harvest)	(strength) (egis)	(hidden) (game)	(defence)	(sun)

Teiwaz	Berkana	Ehwaz	Mannaz	Lagu	Ingwaz	Dægaz	Othala
[T]	[B]	[E,Eh]	[M]	[L]	[-Ing,Ŋ]	[D]	[O/Ω]
tyr	birch	horse	man	lake	ing	day	heritage
(warrior)	(birth)	(wheel/luck)	(human)	(lagoon)	(living)	(dawn)	(estate)

APPENDIX C

THE WHEEL OF THE YEAR

The Sabbats

Imbolc (im'olc)
February 1–2

WORK WITH YOUR ANCESTOR OF MANIFESTATION

Imbolc, when spring is nearly at the door, is celebrated in Ireland as St. Brigid's Day. It's a time of celebration, giving thanks at wells and springs, and cleaning the house and sweeping out the old and stagnant energies.

Brigid was known by many names and faces, including warrior, poet, spring goddess, smith, and healer. Perhaps it's her reputation for healing that caused so many sacred wells to carry her name. This is a season to open yourself to possibility. Like Brigid, fight for yourself and fight for good.

BRIGID'S SPREAD

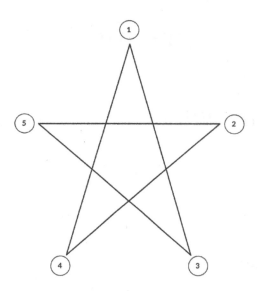

Using your entire deck, shuffle well and then draw five cards.

1. What needs healing?

2. What needs creating?

3. What needs fire?

4. What tiny shoot is pushing up through the snow?

5. What needs to stay frozen?

I don't know if it's Brigid's magic or just happenstance, but this spread is more powerful than I could have imagined. It called me on every bit of my nonsense. Brigid is at work here.

Ostara

March 20

WORK WITH YOUR ANCESTOR OF HEALING

*Behold, my friends, the spring is come; the earth has gladly
received the embraces of the sun, and we shall soon see the results
of their love.*

—SITTING BULL, HUNKPAPA LAKOTA LEADER

Wake up! That's what Mother Earth is doing. Although you may still see the slushy muck of winter's leftovers, spring is here. If any season assures us that the old can be left behind and the slate wiped clean, it's spring.

Even in warmer climates, spring brings an almost ancient need to discard the clutter, clean the closets, sweep the old out the door, and head to the garden. With our windows and doors thrown open, spring enters to clean out the old habits and patterns that have been hiding in winter's fog.

Have you noticed that with spring you leave behind the inner world of reflection and enter the outer world of new growth?

SPRING IN THE LAND OF TAROT

1. Spring cleaning—what to sweep out

2. An ancestor who wants to help me in this season

3. What needs grounding

4. How to ground

5. Outcome of spring energy

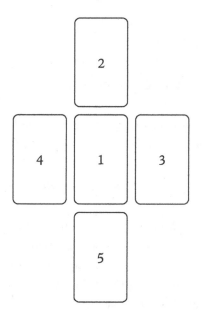

LET ME SHARE THIS

Sometimes ancestral messages seem contradictory, like the cards I drew for positions 1 and 2. Judgement came up as something to sweep out. The message for me is to stop my constant need to rebirth. I know I have a thing about constantly challenging myself, but perhaps I do it too often and too harshly. Noted.

The Knight of Swords was the ancestor who wants to help me. He's the one who is constantly on a quest for exciting and innovative ideas.

Now isn't that rich? Tell me to sweep out my quest for new and then an ancestor comes forward who lives for that quest.

What if you get totally contradictory messages like these? Draw more cards or use your pendulum. There's always guidance for you, and if it's not clear, then doing the spread isn't useful. I drew an oracle to see why I was being told two seemingly contradictory things. My card was a Squirrel. My interpretation was that letting go didn't need to be forever, but it does need to be for now.

SHADOW WORK

If you're doing shadow work, the question for you to draw a single card for is this:

Do you have preconceived notions that obstruct your ability to wipe the old slate clean and begin again?

Beltane

May 1

WORK WITH THE PHASES OF THE MOON

Beltane is a time when mischief is in the air! Young girls dance around the Maypole. Couples drift off into the woods for evenings of lusty delight. And Bacchus is tending bar.

This is the midpoint between spring and summer. Light—both of the sun and of the spirit—is the watchword. Life is in full bloom and worries are left behind.

Beltane's energy is that of love and sexuality, making it a perfect time for handfasting or marriage. If there is one day in the entire year when fun needs to run rampant, it's this day.

Life in all her glory is on display. Live it to your fullest!

LIGHT THE FIRE

This is a perfect time to be rid of whatever is holding you down. Use your tarot or oracle deck—either is perfect. In fact, if you have a nature-themed deck, pull it out for this one today.

1. Where in my life do I need more fun?

2. How am I being too serious?

3. What old pattern needs to go up in flames?

I worked with an animal-themed deck, and not a surprise, the card that came up for needing more fun was Beaver—the workaholic!

No heavy thinking is needed for this spread. Let your intuition run free.

Litha—Summer Solstice

June 21

WORK WITH THE SOLSTICE MAGICIAN

June is the time of the summer solstice. It's the longest day of the year; the sun has reached its furthest point north, and from now until the winter solstice, the days will grow shorter.

A bonfire—a symbol of the sun—is lit on Litha Eve, as celebrants stay up all night to witness the solstice sunrise. Sacred sites like Stonehenge often livestream both the sunrise and sunset on this day.

This is a time of joyful celebration as we welcome the sun at her most powerful. It's also a time to reflect on what you've achieved in the first half of the year. For me, it's also a time to set out plans for the coming six months.

SUMMER SOLSTICE TAROT SPREAD

1. How do I show my light to the world?

2. The theme of the first six months of this year

3. The theme of the next six months

4. What do I need to release as darkness comes earlier?

5. What aspect of myself needs more light?

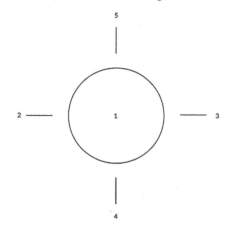

While all my cards for this spread were meaningful, I think the one I most needed to hear was the aspect of self that needs more light. My card was the Queen of Pentacles. I have an embarrassingly long history of terrible self-care. The Queen is stepping in now to take charge.

Lammas

August 1

WORK WITH YOUR PAST LIFE ANCESTOR

Lammas (Lughnasadh) is a cross-quarter day—the time between the summer solstice and the fall equinox. It falls in the last month of summer. Historically Lammas was known as the First Harvest, the time when crops were brought in. For our ancestors, a good harvest versus a bad was the difference between surviving the winter or starving.

In Ireland, the ancient name for Lammas was *Brón Trogain*, "the earth sorrows," so called because the Earth, in giving up her ripe wheat, undergoes the same pain as childbirth.

In August, although the weather is still hot, you can sense the first move toward fall. As with most seasons, the quality of the light begins to change, but now, the nights grow a little longer and daylight shorter. The harvest is a time to count your blessings.

THE HARVEST SPREAD

1. What am I reaping from this season?

2. What chaff can I throw out?

3. What does the earth of my life need for nourishment?

LAMMAS BREAD

I don't love to cook, but I do love to bake. This is my fav bread recipe.

2 cups flour

¾ teaspoon baking soda

½ teaspoon salt

1 cup buttermilk

3 tablespoons melted butter (unsalted)

Combine all the dry ingredients, then add the buttermilk and 2 tablespoons of the butter. At this point I toss it all on some flour and wrestle the whole thing with my bare hands until I've made a rustic-looking loaf that I then top with the remaining tablespoon of butter. About 35 minutes in the oven at 375°F and it's done.

Mabon

September 21

WORK WITH YOUR SKY MAGICIAN

I love September, probably because that's my birthday month. But more than that, I love the subtle change in the light. This occurs because the autumnal equinox falls in September. At this time, the Northern and Southern Hemispheres will receive an equal amount of sunshine. At the South Pole, the sun will finally pop up over the horizon where it will remain for six months. At the North Pole, all will shift into darkness.

The sabbat of Mabon is the second of three harvest festivals (Lammas is the first, Samhain the third). The Catholic Church celebrates Michaelmas, representing the Feast of Saint Michael, around the same time as Mabon. If I could tell you one thing about Mabon, it would be to prepare for an energy shift.

Although you're not ready for winter, you're starting to create your cozy cave. I think of bear, stocking up on fish and berries, putting on the fat needed to sustain her once in hibernation.

Work with Mabon's energy by

⁛ planting tulip and daffodil bulbs

⁛ gathering fruits and veggies you want to can

- collecting fallen leaves for your altar
- baking bread
- making fruit jam
- eating apples or making applesauce or apple butter

THE GATHERER SPREAD

This spread works so well with a nature-themed deck. If you have one, I encourage you to use it for the time of Mabon.

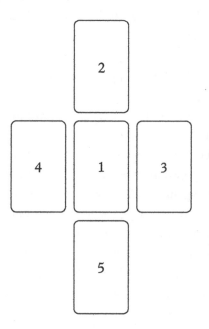

1. What am I most grateful for?
2. What lesson can I learn from others?
3. What part of myself needs reclaiming?
4. What is the state of my personal energy?
5. What do I need to "can" until winter?

Samhain (sow-in)

November 1

WORK WITH YOUR ANCESTOR GUIDE TO THE UNDERWORLD

The sabbat of Samhain begins on October 31 and is often associated with Halloween.

Samhain marks the end of the harvest and the move toward winter. For many cultures, it's the time when communication with the ancestors is at its most potent. If you look at the Wheel of the Year, you'll see that this time of endings is directly opposite Beltane, which is the festival of life and new beginnings.

If there is any sabbat that supports the concept of letting go, this is it. In truth, we do let go at this time of year. We let go of the sun as it moves closer and closer to the south. We let go of growing things and begin to settle into the dark months ahead. At Samhain (as well as Día de los Muertos) we leave food on a plate for the ancestors. We also honor the ancestors through storytelling, keeping them alive in our memories.

This is a time of going inside, reflection, meditation, reviewing the year that came before, and preparing for what comes next. Examine the old patterns that no longer suit you. Let go of habits that you're just beginning to realize have been given too big a part in your life. Face your fears. Learn, correct course, and prepare for what's coming next.

Samhain is the last of the cross-quarter festivals of the year—a point between a solstice and an equinox. Its energy falls in the fixed sign of Scorpio, a Water sign. It is a sign of the psychic, the emotions, and death—so no wonder that Samhain falls within Scorpio's realm. The modern planet that rules Scorpio is Pluto, the god of the Underworld.

THE CHOSEN PATH

Use a tarot deck that feels as though it contains Samhain energy.

1. What is my soul purpose?

2. What do my ancestors think about my path?

3. How can I enrich my soul purpose?

This spread, with only three cards, looks oh-so-simple. But if you dig into each card you draw, you will find a kernel of Samhain energy that you most need on this day.

Yule—Winter Solstice

December 21

WORK WITH YOUR OWN MAGIC

Yule is celebrated on the winter solstice, when the sun has traveled to the far south and the longest night of the year is upon us. This is a time to celebrate, bake cookies, hang greenery, and honor your family and the ancestors. In some traditions, Yule is when the battle between the old year (the Holly King) and the new year (the Oak King) takes place.

The day of the winter solstice is celebrated around the world. Some cultures reenact the holy family seeking refuge in Bethlehem while others consecrate the journey of the Magi, who brought gifts to the Christ child. In the secular world, one culture welcomes Santa with cookies and milk while another puts carrots out for the horse ridden by Sinterklaas.

Regardless of your spiritual path, this is a time for a light in the window and friends around the fire.

YULE SPREAD

Use either your tarot deck or oracle to see what message Yule brings to your doorway.

1. Energy of the old year to release

2. Energy of the new year to embrace

3. My path moving forward

TO OUR READERS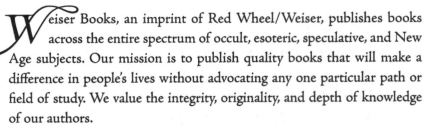